C-1464 CAREER EXAMINATION SERIES

This is your
PASSBOOK for...

Secretarial Assistant

Test Preparation Study Guide
Questions & Answers

COPYRIGHT NOTICE

This book is SOLELY intended for, is sold ONLY to, and its use is RESTRICTED to individual, bona fide applicants or candidates who qualify by virtue of having seriously filed applications for appropriate license, certificate, professional and/or promotional advancement, higher school matriculation, scholarship, or other legitimate requirements of education and/or governmental authorities.

This book is NOT intended for use, class instruction, tutoring, training, duplication, copying, reprinting, excerption, or adaptation, etc., by:

1) Other publishers
2) Proprietors and/or Instructors of "Coaching" and/or Preparatory Courses
3) Personnel and/or Training Divisions of commercial, industrial, and governmental organizations
4) Schools, colleges, or universities and/or their departments and staffs, including teachers and other personnel
5) Testing Agencies or Bureaus
6) Study groups which seek by the purchase of a single volume to copy and/or duplicate and/or adapt this material for use by the group as a whole without having purchased individual volumes for each of the members of the group
7) Et al.

Such persons would be in violation of appropriate Federal and State statutes.

PROVISION OF LICENSING AGREEMENTS – Recognized educational, commercial, industrial, and governmental institutions and organizations, and others legitimately engaged in educational pursuits, including training, testing, and measurement activities, may address request for a licensing agreement to the copyright owners, who will determine whether, and under what conditions, including fees and charges, the materials in this book may be used them. In other words, a licensing facility exists for the legitimate use of the material in this book on other than an individual basis. However, it is asseverated and affirmed here that the material in this book CANNOT be used without the receipt of the express permission of such a licensing agreement from the Publishers. Inquiries re licensing should be addressed to the company, attention rights and permissions department.

All rights reserved, including the right of reproduction in whole or in part, in any form or by any means, electronic or mechanical, including photocopying, recording, or by any information storage and retrieval system, without permission in writing from the Publisher.

Copyright © 2025 by
National Learning Corporation

212 Michael Drive, Syosset, NY 11791
(516) 921-8888 • www.passbooks.com
E-mail: info@passbooks.com

PASSBOOK® SERIES

THE *PASSBOOK® SERIES* has been created to prepare applicants and candidates for the ultimate academic battlefield – the examination room.

At some time in our lives, each and every one of us may be required to take an examination – for validation, matriculation, admission, qualification, registration, certification, or licensure.

Based on the assumption that every applicant or candidate has met the basic formal educational standards, has taken the required number of courses, and read the necessary texts, the *PASSBOOK® SERIES* furnishes the one special preparation which may assure passing with confidence, instead of failing with insecurity. Examination questions – together with answers – are furnished as the basic vehicle for study so that the mysteries of the examination and its compounding difficulties may be eliminated or diminished by a sure method.

This book is meant to help you pass your examination provided that you qualify and are serious in your objective.

The entire field is reviewed through the huge store of content information which is succinctly presented through a provocative and challenging approach – the question-and-answer method.

A climate of success is established by furnishing the correct answers at the end of each test.

You soon learn to recognize types of questions, forms of questions, and patterns of questioning. You may even begin to anticipate expected outcomes.

You perceive that many questions are repeated or adapted so that you can gain acute insights, which may enable you to score many sure points.

You learn how to confront new questions, or types of questions, and to attack them confidently and work out the correct answers.

You note objectives and emphases, and recognize pitfalls and dangers, so that you may make positive educational adjustments.

Moreover, you are kept fully informed in relation to new concepts, methods, practices, and directions in the field.

You discover that you are actually taking the examination all the time: you are preparing for the examination by "taking" an examination, not by reading extraneous and/or supererogatory textbooks.

In short, this PASSBOOK®, used directedly, should be an important factor in helping you to pass your test.

SECRETARIAL ASSISTANT

DUTIES

An employee in this class performs secretarial work with administrative or highly technical responsibilities. Work is generally performed for the head of a major department or division and involves confidential and complex clerical tasks requiring independent judgment and action. Duties may include supervision over supervisory or other clerical personnel engaged in routine office operations. The employee, if qualified, may be asked to take dictation, but stenographic skill is not a requirement for positions in the class. The employee may relieve the department head of routine management, personnel and payroll details and/or perform highly specialized and technical clerical activities under general supervision. Employees are responsible for the proper performance of the assigned supervisory or technical activities of their unit and make independent work decisions based on long experience and thorough knowledge of departmental operations. Highly difficult technical, policy or procedural questions are referred to the department head for decision. Work is reviewed through frequent consultations with the administrative head and by examination of work performed. Does related work as required.

SCOPE OF THE EXAMINATION

The written test will cover knowledge, skills, and/or abilities in such areas as:
1. Secretarial practices;
2. Understanding and interpreting written material;
3. English usage, sentence structure, grammar, spelling, and punctuation;
4. Basic computer usage;
5. Interpreting data in record keeping; and
6. Clerical operations.

HOW TO TAKE A TEST

I. YOU MUST PASS AN EXAMINATION

A. WHAT EVERY CANDIDATE SHOULD KNOW

Examination applicants often ask us for help in preparing for the written test. What can I study in advance? What kinds of questions will be asked? How will the test be given? How will the papers be graded?

As an applicant for a civil service examination, you may be wondering about some of these things. Our purpose here is to suggest effective methods of advance study and to describe civil service examinations.

Your chances for success on this examination can be increased if you know how to prepare. Those "pre-examination jitters" can be reduced if you know what to expect. You can even experience an adventure in good citizenship if you know why civil service exams are given.

B. WHY ARE CIVIL SERVICE EXAMINATIONS GIVEN?

Civil service examinations are important to you in two ways. As a citizen, you want public jobs filled by employees who know how to do their work. As a job seeker, you want a fair chance to compete for that job on an equal footing with other candidates. The best-known means of accomplishing this two-fold goal is the competitive examination.

Exams are widely publicized throughout the nation. They may be administered for jobs in federal, state, city, municipal, town or village governments or agencies.

Any citizen may apply, with some limitations, such as the age or residence of applicants. Your experience and education may be reviewed to see whether you meet the requirements for the particular examination. When these requirements exist, they are reasonable and applied consistently to all applicants. Thus, a competitive examination may cause you some uneasiness now, but it is your privilege and safeguard.

C. HOW ARE CIVIL SERVICE EXAMS DEVELOPED?

Examinations are carefully written by trained technicians who are specialists in the field known as "psychological measurement," in consultation with recognized authorities in the field of work that the test will cover. These experts recommend the subject matter areas or skills to be tested; only those knowledges or skills important to your success on the job are included. The most reliable books and source materials available are used as references. Together, the experts and technicians judge the difficulty level of the questions.

Test technicians know how to phrase questions so that the problem is clearly stated. Their ethics do not permit "trick" or "catch" questions. Questions may have been tried out on sample groups, or subjected to statistical analysis, to determine their usefulness.

Written tests are often used in combination with performance tests, ratings of training and experience, and oral interviews. All of these measures combine to form the best-known means of finding the right person for the right job.

II. HOW TO PASS THE WRITTEN TEST

A. NATURE OF THE EXAMINATION

To prepare intelligently for civil service examinations, you should know how they differ from school examinations you have taken. In school you were assigned certain definite pages to read or subjects to cover. The examination questions were quite detailed and usually emphasized memory. Civil service exams, on the other hand, try to discover your present ability to perform the duties of a position, plus your potentiality to learn these duties. In other words, a civil service exam attempts to predict how successful you will be. Questions cover such a broad area that they cannot be as minute and detailed as school exam questions.

In the public service similar kinds of work, or positions, are grouped together in one "class." This process is known as *position-classification*. All the positions in a class are paid according to the salary range for that class. One class title covers all of these positions, and they are all tested by the same examination.

B. FOUR BASIC STEPS

1) Study the announcement

How, then, can you know what subjects to study? Our best answer is: "Learn as much as possible about the class of positions for which you've applied." The exam will test the knowledge, skills and abilities needed to do the work.

Your most valuable source of information about the position you want is the official exam announcement. This announcement lists the training and experience qualifications. Check these standards and apply only if you come reasonably close to meeting them.

The brief description of the position in the examination announcement offers some clues to the subjects which will be tested. Think about the job itself. Review the duties in your mind. Can you perform them, or are there some in which you are rusty? Fill in the blank spots in your preparation.

Many jurisdictions preview the written test in the exam announcement by including a section called "Knowledge and Abilities Required," "Scope of the Examination," or some similar heading. Here you will find out specifically what fields will be tested.

2) Review your own background

Once you learn in general what the position is all about, and what you need to know to do the work, ask yourself which subjects you already know fairly well and which need improvement. You may wonder whether to concentrate on improving your strong areas or on building some background in your fields of weakness. When the announcement has specified "some knowledge" or "considerable knowledge," or has used adjectives like "beginning principles of…" or "advanced … methods," you can get a clue as to the number and difficulty of questions to be asked in any given field. More questions, and hence broader coverage, would be included for those subjects which are more important in the work. Now weigh your strengths and weaknesses against the job requirements and prepare accordingly.

3) Determine the level of the position

Another way to tell how intensively you should prepare is to understand the level of the job for which you are applying. Is it the entering level? In other words, is this the position in which beginners in a field of work are hired? Or is it an intermediate or advanced level? Sometimes this is indicated by such words as "Junior" or "Senior" in the class title. Other jurisdictions use Roman numerals to designate the level – Clerk I, Clerk II, for example. The word "Supervisor" sometimes appears in the title. If the level is not indicated by the title, check the description of duties. Will you be working under very close supervision, or will you have responsibility for independent decisions in this work?

4) Choose appropriate study materials

Now that you know the subjects to be examined and the relative amount of each subject to be covered, you can choose suitable study materials. For beginning level jobs, or even advanced ones, if you have a pronounced weakness in some aspect of your training, read a modern, standard textbook in that field. Be sure it is up to date and has general coverage. Such books are normally available at your library, and the librarian will be glad to help you locate one. For entry-level positions, questions of appropriate difficulty are chosen – neither highly advanced questions, nor those too simple. Such questions require careful thought but not advanced training.

If the position for which you are applying is technical or advanced, you will read more advanced, specialized material. If you are already familiar with the basic principles of your field, elementary textbooks would waste your time. Concentrate on advanced textbooks and technical periodicals. Think through the concepts and review difficult problems in your field.

These are all general sources. You can get more ideas on your own initiative, following these leads. For example, training manuals and publications of the government agency which employs workers in your field can be useful, particularly for technical and professional positions. A letter or visit to the government department involved may result in more specific study suggestions, and certainly will provide you with a more definite idea of the exact nature of the position you are seeking.

III. KINDS OF TESTS

Tests are used for purposes other than measuring knowledge and ability to perform specified duties. For some positions, it is equally important to test ability to make adjustments to new situations or to profit from training. In others, basic mental abilities not dependent on information are essential. Questions which test these things may not appear as pertinent to the duties of the position as those which test for knowledge and information. Yet they are often highly important parts of a fair examination. For very general questions, it is almost impossible to help you direct your study efforts. What we can do is to point out some of the more common of these general abilities needed in public service positions and describe some typical questions.

1) General information

Broad, general information has been found useful for predicting job success in some kinds of work. This is tested in a variety of ways, from vocabulary lists to questions about current events. Basic background in some field of work, such as sociology or economics, may be sampled in a group of questions. Often these are principles which have become familiar to most persons through exposure rather than through formal training. It is difficult to advise you how to study for these questions; being alert to the world around you is our best suggestion.

2) Verbal ability

An example of an ability needed in many positions is verbal or language ability. Verbal ability is, in brief, the ability to use and understand words. Vocabulary and grammar tests are typical measures of this ability. Reading comprehension or paragraph interpretation questions are common in many kinds of civil service tests. You are given a paragraph of written material and asked to find its central meaning.

3) Numerical ability

Number skills can be tested by the familiar arithmetic problem, by checking paired lists of numbers to see which are alike and which are different, or by interpreting charts and graphs. In the latter test, a graph may be printed in the test booklet which you are asked to use as the basis for answering questions.

4) Observation

A popular test for law-enforcement positions is the observation test. A picture is shown to you for several minutes, then taken away. Questions about the picture test your ability to observe both details and larger elements.

5) Following directions

In many positions in the public service, the employee must be able to carry out written instructions dependably and accurately. You may be given a chart with several columns, each column listing a variety of information. The questions require you to carry out directions involving the information given in the chart.

6) Skills and aptitudes

Performance tests effectively measure some manual skills and aptitudes. When the skill is one in which you are trained, such as typing or shorthand, you can practice. These tests are often very much like those given in business school or high school courses. For many of the other skills and aptitudes, however, no short-time preparation can be made. Skills and abilities natural to you or that you have developed throughout your lifetime are being tested.

Many of the general questions just described provide all the data needed to answer the questions and ask you to use your reasoning ability to find the answers. Your best preparation for these tests, as well as for tests of facts and ideas, is to be at your physical and mental best. You, no doubt, have your own methods of getting into an exam-taking mood and keeping "in shape." The next section lists some ideas on this subject.

IV. KINDS OF QUESTIONS

Only rarely is the "essay" question, which you answer in narrative form, used in civil service tests. Civil service tests are usually of the short-answer type. Full instructions for answering these questions will be given to you at the examination. But in case this is your first experience with short-answer questions and separate answer sheets, here is what you need to know:

1) **Multiple-choice Questions**

Most popular of the short-answer questions is the "multiple choice" or "best answer" question. It can be used, for example, to test for factual knowledge, ability to solve problems or judgment in meeting situations found at work.

A multiple-choice question is normally one of three types—
- It can begin with an incomplete statement followed by several possible endings. You are to find the one ending which *best* completes the statement, although some of the others may not be entirely wrong.
- It can also be a complete statement in the form of a question which is answered by choosing one of the statements listed.

- It can be in the form of a problem – again you select the best answer.

Here is an example of a multiple-choice question with a discussion which should give you some clues as to the method for choosing the right answer:

When an employee has a complaint about his assignment, the action which will *best* help him overcome his difficulty is to
    A. discuss his difficulty with his coworkers
    B. take the problem to the head of the organization
    C. take the problem to the person who gave him the assignment
    D. say nothing to anyone about his complaint

In answering this question, you should study each of the choices to find which is best. Consider choice "A" – Certainly an employee may discuss his complaint with fellow employees, but no change or improvement can result, and the complaint remains unresolved. Choice "B" is a poor choice since the head of the organization probably does not know what assignment you have been given, and taking your problem to him is known as "going over the head" of the supervisor. The supervisor, or person who made the assignment, is the person who can clarify it or correct any injustice. Choice "C" is, therefore, correct. To say nothing, as in choice "D," is unwise. Supervisors have and interest in knowing the problems employees are facing, and the employee is seeking a solution to his problem.

2) True/False Questions

The "true/false" or "right/wrong" form of question is sometimes used. Here a complete statement is given. Your job is to decide whether the statement is right or wrong.

SAMPLE: A roaming cell-phone call to a nearby city costs less than a non-roaming call to a distant city.

This statement is wrong, or false, since roaming calls are more expensive.

This is not a complete list of all possible question forms, although most of the others are variations of these common types. You will always get complete directions for answering questions. Be sure you understand *how* to mark your answers – ask questions until you do.

V. RECORDING YOUR ANSWERS

Computer terminals are used more and more today for many different kinds of exams.
For an examination with very few applicants, you may be told to record your answers in the test booklet itself. Separate answer sheets are much more common. If this separate answer sheet is to be scored by machine – and this is often the case – it is highly important that you mark your answers correctly in order to get credit.

An electronic scoring machine is often used in civil service offices because of the speed with which papers can be scored. Machine-scored answer sheets must be marked with a pencil, which will be given to you. This pencil has a high graphite content which responds to the electronic scoring machine. As a matter of fact, stray dots may register as answers, so do not let your pencil rest on the answer sheet while you are pondering the correct answer. Also, if your pencil lead breaks or is otherwise defective, ask for another.

Since the answer sheet will be dropped in a slot in the scoring machine, be careful not to bend the corners or get the paper crumpled.

The answer sheet normally has five vertical columns of numbers, with 30 numbers to a column. These numbers correspond to the question numbers in your test booklet. After each number, going across the page are four or five pairs of dotted lines. These short dotted lines have small letters or numbers above them. The first two pairs may also have a "T" or "F" above the letters. This indicates that the first two pairs only are to be used if the questions are of the true-false type. If the questions are multiple choice, disregard the "T" and "F" and pay attention only to the small letters or numbers.

Answer your questions in the manner of the sample that follows:

32. The largest city in the United States is
    A. Washington, D.C.
    B. New York City
    C. Chicago
    D. Detroit
    E. San Francisco

1) Choose the answer you think is best. (New York City is the largest, so "B" is correct.)
2) Find the row of dotted lines numbered the same as the question you are answering. (Find row number 32)
3) Find the pair of dotted lines corresponding to the answer. (Find the pair of lines under the mark "B.")
4) Make a solid black mark between the dotted lines.

VI. BEFORE THE TEST

Common sense will help you find procedures to follow to get ready for an examination. Too many of us, however, overlook these sensible measures. Indeed, nervousness and fatigue have been found to be the most serious reasons why applicants fail to do their best on civil service tests. Here is a list of reminders:

- Begin your preparation early – Don't wait until the last minute to go scurrying around for books and materials or to find out what the position is all about.
- Prepare continuously – An hour a night for a week is better than an all-night cram session. This has been definitely established. What is more, a night a week for a month will return better dividends than crowding your study into a shorter period of time.
- Locate the place of the exam – You have been sent a notice telling you when and where to report for the examination. If the location is in a different town or otherwise unfamiliar to you, it would be well to inquire the best route and learn something about the building.
- Relax the night before the test – Allow your mind to rest. Do not study at all that night. Plan some mild recreation or diversion; then go to bed early and get a good night's sleep.
- Get up early enough to make a leisurely trip to the place for the test – This way unforeseen events, traffic snarls, unfamiliar buildings, etc. will not upset you.
- Dress comfortably – A written test is not a fashion show. You will be known by number and not by name, so wear something comfortable.

- Leave excess paraphernalia at home – Shopping bags and odd bundles will get in your way. You need bring only the items mentioned in the official notice you received; usually everything you need is provided. Do not bring reference books to the exam. They will only confuse those last minutes and be taken away from you when in the test room.
- Arrive somewhat ahead of time – If because of transportation schedules you must get there very early, bring a newspaper or magazine to take your mind off yourself while waiting.
- Locate the examination room – When you have found the proper room, you will be directed to the seat or part of the room where you will sit. Sometimes you are given a sheet of instructions to read while you are waiting. Do not fill out any forms until you are told to do so; just read them and be prepared.
- Relax and prepare to listen to the instructions
- If you have any physical problem that may keep you from doing your best, be sure to tell the test administrator. If you are sick or in poor health, you really cannot do your best on the exam. You can come back and take the test some other time.

VII. AT THE TEST

The day of the test is here and you have the test booklet in your hand. The temptation to get going is very strong. Caution! There is more to success than knowing the right answers. You must know how to identify your papers and understand variations in the type of short-answer question used in this particular examination. Follow these suggestions for maximum results from your efforts:

1) Cooperate with the monitor

The test administrator has a duty to create a situation in which you can be as much at ease as possible. He will give instructions, tell you when to begin, check to see that you are marking your answer sheet correctly, and so on. He is not there to guard you, although he will see that your competitors do not take unfair advantage. He wants to help you do your best.

2) Listen to all instructions

Don't jump the gun! Wait until you understand all directions. In most civil service tests you get more time than you need to answer the questions. So don't be in a hurry. Read each word of instructions until you clearly understand the meaning. Study the examples, listen to all announcements and follow directions. Ask questions if you do not understand what to do.

3) Identify your papers

Civil service exams are usually identified by number only. You will be assigned a number; you must not put your name on your test papers. Be sure to copy your number correctly. Since more than one exam may be given, copy your exact examination title.

4) Plan your time

Unless you are told that a test is a "speed" or "rate of work" test, speed itself is usually not important. Time enough to answer all the questions will be provided, but this does not mean that you have all day. An overall time limit has been set. Divide the total time (in minutes) by the number of questions to determine the approximate time you have for each question.

5) Do not linger over difficult questions

If you come across a difficult question, mark it with a paper clip (useful to have along) and come back to it when you have been through the booklet. One caution if you do this – be sure to skip a number on your answer sheet as well. Check often to be sure that you have not lost your place and that you are marking in the row numbered the same as the question you are answering.

6) Read the questions

Be sure you know what the question asks! Many capable people are unsuccessful because they failed to *read* the questions correctly.

7) Answer all questions

Unless you have been instructed that a penalty will be deducted for incorrect answers, it is better to guess than to omit a question.

8) Speed tests

It is often better NOT to guess on speed tests. It has been found that on timed tests people are tempted to spend the last few seconds before time is called in marking answers at random – without even reading them – in the hope of picking up a few extra points. To discourage this practice, the instructions may warn you that your score will be "corrected" for guessing. That is, a penalty will be applied. The incorrect answers will be deducted from the correct ones, or some other penalty formula will be used.

9) Review your answers

If you finish before time is called, go back to the questions you guessed or omitted to give them further thought. Review other answers if you have time.

10) Return your test materials

If you are ready to leave before others have finished or time is called, take ALL your materials to the monitor and leave quietly. Never take any test material with you. The monitor can discover whose papers are not complete, and taking a test booklet may be grounds for disqualification.

VIII. EXAMINATION TECHNIQUES

1) Read the general instructions carefully. These are usually printed on the first page of the exam booklet. As a rule, these instructions refer to the timing of the examination; the fact that you should not start work until the signal and must stop work at a signal, etc. If there are any *special* instructions, such as a choice of questions to be answered, make sure that you note this instruction carefully.

2) When you are ready to start work on the examination, that is as soon as the signal has been given, read the instructions to each question booklet, underline any key words or phrases, such as *least, best, outline, describe* and the like. In this way you will tend to answer as requested rather than discover on reviewing your paper that you *listed without describing*, that you selected the *worst* choice rather than the *best* choice, etc.

3) If the examination is of the objective or multiple-choice type – that is, each question will also give a series of possible answers: A, B, C or D, and you are called upon to select the best answer and write the letter next to that answer on your answer paper – it is advisable to start answering each question in turn. There may be anywhere from 50 to 100 such questions in the three or four hours allotted and you can see how much time would be taken if you read through all the questions before beginning to answer any. Furthermore, if you come across a question or group of questions which you know would be difficult to answer, it would undoubtedly affect your handling of all the other questions.

4) If the examination is of the essay type and contains but a few questions, it is a moot point as to whether you should read all the questions before starting to answer any one. Of course, if you are given a choice – say five out of seven and the like – then it is essential to read all the questions so you can eliminate the two that are most difficult. If, however, you are asked to answer all the questions, there may be danger in trying to answer the easiest one first because you may find that you will spend too much time on it. The best technique is to answer the first question, then proceed to the second, etc.

5) Time your answers. Before the exam begins, write down the time it started, then add the time allowed for the examination and write down the time it must be completed, then divide the time available somewhat as follows:
    - If 3-1/2 hours are allowed, that would be 210 minutes. If you have 80 objective-type questions, that would be an average of 2-1/2 minutes per question. Allow yourself no more than 2 minutes per question, or a total of 160 minutes, which will permit about 50 minutes to review.
    - If for the time allotment of 210 minutes there are 7 essay questions to answer, that would average about 30 minutes a question. Give yourself only 25 minutes per question so that you have about 35 minutes to review.

6) The most important instruction is to *read each question* and make sure you know what is wanted. The second most important instruction is to *time yourself properly* so that you answer every question. The third most important instruction is to *answer every question*. Guess if you have to but include something for each question. Remember that you will receive no credit for a blank and will probably receive some credit if you write something in answer to an essay question. If you guess a letter – say "B" for a multiple-choice question – you may have guessed right. If you leave a blank as an answer to a multiple-choice question, the examiners may respect your feelings but it will not add a point to your score. Some exams may penalize you for wrong answers, so in such cases *only*, you may not want to guess unless you have some basis for your answer.

7) Suggestions
    a. Objective-type questions
        1. Examine the question booklet for proper sequence of pages and questions
        2. Read all instructions carefully
        3. Skip any question which seems too difficult; return to it after all other questions have been answered
        4. Apportion your time properly; do not spend too much time on any single question or group of questions

5. Note and underline key words – *all, most, fewest, least, best, worst, same, opposite,* etc.
6. Pay particular attention to negatives
7. Note unusual option, e.g., unduly long, short, complex, different or similar in content to the body of the question
8. Observe the use of "hedging" words – *probably, may, most likely,* etc.
9. Make sure that your answer is put next to the same number as the question
10. Do not second-guess unless you have good reason to believe the second answer is definitely more correct
11. Cross out original answer if you decide another answer is more accurate; do not erase until you are ready to hand your paper in
12. Answer all questions; guess unless instructed otherwise
13. Leave time for review

b. Essay questions
   1. Read each question carefully
   2. Determine exactly what is wanted. Underline key words or phrases.
   3. Decide on outline or paragraph answer
   4. Include many different points and elements unless asked to develop any one or two points or elements
   5. Show impartiality by giving pros and cons unless directed to select one side only
   6. Make and write down any assumptions you find necessary to answer the questions
   7. Watch your English, grammar, punctuation and choice of words
   8. Time your answers; don't crowd material

8) Answering the essay question

Most essay questions can be answered by framing the specific response around several key words or ideas. Here are a few such key words or ideas:

M's: manpower, materials, methods, money, management
P's: purpose, program, policy, plan, procedure, practice, problems, pitfalls, personnel, public relations

   a. Six basic steps in handling problems:
      1. Preliminary plan and background development
      2. Collect information, data and facts
      3. Analyze and interpret information, data and facts
      4. Analyze and develop solutions as well as make recommendations
      5. Prepare report and sell recommendations
      6. Install recommendations and follow up effectiveness

   b. Pitfalls to avoid
      1. *Taking things for granted* – A statement of the situation does not necessarily imply that each of the elements is necessarily true; for example, a complaint may be invalid and biased so that all that can be taken for granted is that a complaint has been registered

2. *Considering only one side of a situation* – Wherever possible, indicate several alternatives and then point out the reasons you selected the best one
3. *Failing to indicate follow up* – Whenever your answer indicates action on your part, make certain that you will take proper follow-up action to see how successful your recommendations, procedures or actions turn out to be
4. *Taking too long in answering any single question* – Remember to time your answers properly

IX. AFTER THE TEST

Scoring procedures differ in detail among civil service jurisdictions although the general principles are the same. Whether the papers are hand-scored or graded by machine we have described, they are nearly always graded by number. That is, the person who marks the paper knows only the number – never the name – of the applicant. Not until all the papers have been graded will they be matched with names. If other tests, such as training and experience or oral interview ratings have been given, scores will be combined. Different parts of the examination usually have different weights. For example, the written test might count 60 percent of the final grade, and a rating of training and experience 40 percent. In many jurisdictions, veterans will have a certain number of points added to their grades.

After the final grade has been determined, the names are placed in grade order and an eligible list is established. There are various methods for resolving ties between those who get the same final grade – probably the most common is to place first the name of the person whose application was received first. Job offers are made from the eligible list in the order the names appear on it. You will be notified of your grade and your rank as soon as all these computations have been made. This will be done as rapidly as possible.

People who are found to meet the requirements in the announcement are called "eligibles." Their names are put on a list of eligible candidates. An eligible's chances of getting a job depend on how high he stands on this list and how fast agencies are filling jobs from the list.

When a job is to be filled from a list of eligibles, the agency asks for the names of people on the list of eligibles for that job. When the civil service commission receives this request, it sends to the agency the names of the three people highest on this list. Or, if the job to be filled has specialized requirements, the office sends the agency the names of the top three persons who meet these requirements from the general list.

The appointing officer makes a choice from among the three people whose names were sent to him. If the selected person accepts the appointment, the names of the others are put back on the list to be considered for future openings.

That is the rule in hiring from all kinds of eligible lists, whether they are for typist, carpenter, chemist, or something else. For every vacancy, the appointing officer has his choice of any one of the top three eligibles on the list. This explains why the person whose name is on top of the list sometimes does not get an appointment when some of the persons lower on the list do. If the appointing officer chooses the second or third eligible, the No. 1 eligible does not get a job at once, but stays on the list until he is appointed or the list is terminated.

X. HOW TO PASS THE INTERVIEW TEST

The examination for which you applied requires an oral interview test. You have already taken the written test and you are now being called for the interview test – the final part of the formal examination.

You may think that it is not possible to prepare for an interview test and that there are no procedures to follow during an interview. Our purpose is to point out some things you can do in advance that will help you and some good rules to follow and pitfalls to avoid while you are being interviewed.

What is an interview supposed to test?

The written examination is designed to test the technical knowledge and competence of the candidate; the oral is designed to evaluate intangible qualities, not readily measured otherwise, and to establish a list showing the relative fitness of each candidate – as measured against his competitors – for the position sought. Scoring is not on the basis of "right" and "wrong," but on a sliding scale of values ranging from "not passable" to "outstanding." As a matter of fact, it is possible to achieve a relatively low score without a single "incorrect" answer because of evident weakness in the qualities being measured.

Occasionally, an examination may consist entirely of an oral test – either an individual or a group oral. In such cases, information is sought concerning the technical knowledges and abilities of the candidate, since there has been no written examination for this purpose. More commonly, however, an oral test is used to supplement a written examination.

Who conducts interviews?

The composition of oral boards varies among different jurisdictions. In nearly all, a representative of the personnel department serves as chairman. One of the members of the board may be a representative of the department in which the candidate would work. In some cases, "outside experts" are used, and, frequently, a businessman or some other representative of the general public is asked to serve. Labor and management or other special groups may be represented. The aim is to secure the services of experts in the appropriate field.

However the board is composed, it is a good idea (and not at all improper or unethical) to ascertain in advance of the interview who the members are and what groups they represent. When you are introduced to them, you will have some idea of their backgrounds and interests, and at least you will not stutter and stammer over their names.

What should be done before the interview?

While knowledge about the board members is useful and takes some of the surprise element out of the interview, there is other preparation which is more substantive. It *is* possible to prepare for an oral interview – in several ways:

1) Keep a copy of your application and review it carefully before the interview

This may be the only document before the oral board, and the starting point of the interview. Know what education and experience you have listed there, and the sequence and dates of all of it. Sometimes the board will ask you to review the highlights of your experience for them; you should not have to hem and haw doing it.

2) Study the class specification and the examination announcement

Usually, the oral board has one or both of these to guide them. The qualities, characteristics or knowledges required by the position sought are stated in these documents. They offer valuable clues as to the nature of the oral interview. For example, if the job involves supervisory responsibilities, the announcement will usually indicate that knowledge of modern supervisory methods and the qualifications of the candidate as a supervisor will be tested. If so, you can expect such questions, frequently in the form of a hypothetical situation which you are expected to solve. NEVER go into an oral without knowledge of the duties and responsibilities of the job you seek.

3) Think through each qualification required

Try to visualize the kind of questions you would ask if you were a board member. How well could you answer them? Try especially to appraise your own knowledge and background in each area, *measured against the job sought*, and identify any areas in which you are weak. Be critical and realistic – do not flatter yourself.

4) Do some general reading in areas in which you feel you may be weak

For example, if the job involves supervision and your past experience has NOT, some general reading in supervisory methods and practices, particularly in the field of human relations, might be useful. Do NOT study agency procedures or detailed manuals. The oral board will be testing your understanding and capacity, not your memory.

5) Get a good night's sleep and watch your general health and mental attitude

You will want a clear head at the interview. Take care of a cold or any other minor ailment, and of course, no hangovers.

What should be done on the day of the interview?

Now comes the day of the interview itself. Give yourself plenty of time to get there. Plan to arrive somewhat ahead of the scheduled time, particularly if your appointment is in the fore part of the day. If a previous candidate fails to appear, the board might be ready for you a bit early. By early afternoon an oral board is almost invariably behind schedule if there are many candidates, and you may have to wait. Take along a book or magazine to read, or your application to review, but leave any extraneous material in the waiting room when you go in for your interview. In any event, relax and compose yourself.

The matter of dress is important. The board is forming impressions about you – from your experience, your manners, your attitude, and your appearance. Give your personal appearance careful attention. Dress your best, but not your flashiest. Choose conservative, appropriate clothing, and be sure it is immaculate. This is a business interview, and your appearance should indicate that you regard it as such. Besides, being well groomed and properly dressed will help boost your confidence.

Sooner or later, someone will call your name and escort you into the interview room. *This is it.* From here on you are on your own. It is too late for any more preparation. But remember, you asked for this opportunity to prove your fitness, and you are here because your request was granted.

What happens when you go in?

The usual sequence of events will be as follows: The clerk (who is often the board stenographer) will introduce you to the chairman of the oral board, who will introduce you to the other members of the board. Acknowledge the introductions before you sit down. Do not be surprised if you find a microphone facing you or a stenotypist sitting by. Oral interviews are usually recorded in the event of an appeal or other review.

Usually the chairman of the board will open the interview by reviewing the highlights of your education and work experience from your application – primarily for the benefit of the other members of the board, as well as to get the material into the record. Do not interrupt or comment unless there is an error or significant misinterpretation; if that is the case, do not hesitate. But do not quibble about insignificant matters. Also, he will usually ask you some question about your education, experience or your present job – partly to get you to start talking and to establish the interviewing "rapport." He may start the actual questioning, or turn it over to one of the other members. Frequently, each member undertakes the questioning on a particular area, one in which he is perhaps most competent, so you can expect each member to participate in the examination. Because time is limited, you may also expect some rather abrupt switches in the direction the questioning takes, so do not be upset by it. Normally, a board member will not pursue a single line of questioning unless he discovers a particular strength or weakness.

After each member has participated, the chairman will usually ask whether any member has any further questions, then will ask you if you have anything you wish to add. Unless you are expecting this question, it may floor you. Worse, it may start you off on an extended, extemporaneous speech. The board is not usually seeking more information. The question is principally to offer you a last opportunity to present further qualifications or to indicate that you have nothing to add. So, if you feel that a significant qualification or characteristic has been overlooked, it is proper to point it out in a sentence or so. Do not compliment the board on the thoroughness of their examination – they have been sketchy, and you know it. If you wish, merely say, "No thank you, I have nothing further to add." This is a point where you can "talk yourself out" of a good impression or fail to present an important bit of information. Remember, *you close the interview yourself*.

The chairman will then say, "That is all, Mr. _____, thank you." Do not be startled; the interview is over, and quicker than you think. Thank him, gather your belongings and take your leave. Save your sigh of relief for the other side of the door.

How to put your best foot forward

Throughout this entire process, you may feel that the board individually and collectively is trying to pierce your defenses, seek out your hidden weaknesses and embarrass and confuse you. Actually, this is not true. They are obliged to make an appraisal of your qualifications for the job you are seeking, and they want to see you in your best light. Remember, they must interview all candidates and a non-cooperative candidate may become a failure in spite of their best efforts to bring out his qualifications. Here are 15 suggestions that will help you:

1) Be natural – Keep your attitude confident, not cocky

If you are not confident that you can do the job, do not expect the board to be. Do not apologize for your weaknesses, try to bring out your strong points. The board is interested in a positive, not negative, presentation. Cockiness will antagonize any board member and make him wonder if you are covering up a weakness by a false show of strength.

2) Get comfortable, but don't lounge or sprawl

Sit erectly but not stiffly. A careless posture may lead the board to conclude that you are careless in other things, or at least that you are not impressed by the importance of the occasion. Either conclusion is natural, even if incorrect. Do not fuss with your clothing, a pencil or an ashtray. Your hands may occasionally be useful to emphasize a point; do not let them become a point of distraction.

3) Do not wisecrack or make small talk

This is a serious situation, and your attitude should show that you consider it as such. Further, the time of the board is limited – they do not want to waste it, and neither should you.

4) Do not exaggerate your experience or abilities

In the first place, from information in the application or other interviews and sources, the board may know more about you than you think. Secondly, you probably will not get away with it. An experienced board is rather adept at spotting such a situation, so do not take the chance.

5) If you know a board member, do not make a point of it, yet do not hide it

Certainly you are not fooling him, and probably not the other members of the board. Do not try to take advantage of your acquaintanceship – it will probably do you little good.

6) Do not dominate the interview

Let the board do that. They will give you the clues – do not assume that you have to do all the talking. Realize that the board has a number of questions to ask you, and do not try to take up all the interview time by showing off your extensive knowledge of the answer to the first one.

7) Be attentive

You only have 20 minutes or so, and you should keep your attention at its sharpest throughout. When a member is addressing a problem or question to you, give him your undivided attention. Address your reply principally to him, but do not exclude the other board members.

8) Do not interrupt

A board member may be stating a problem for you to analyze. He will ask you a question when the time comes. Let him state the problem, and wait for the question.

9) Make sure you understand the question

Do not try to answer until you are sure what the question is. If it is not clear, restate it in your own words or ask the board member to clarify it for you. However, do not haggle about minor elements.

10) Reply promptly but not hastily

A common entry on oral board rating sheets is "candidate responded readily," or "candidate hesitated in replies." Respond as promptly and quickly as you can, but do not jump to a hasty, ill-considered answer.

11) Do not be peremptory in your answers

A brief answer is proper – but do not fire your answer back. That is a losing game from your point of view. The board member can probably ask questions much faster than you can answer them.

12) Do not try to create the answer you think the board member wants

He is interested in what kind of mind you have and how it works – not in playing games. Furthermore, he can usually spot this practice and will actually grade you down on it.

13) Do not switch sides in your reply merely to agree with a board member

Frequently, a member will take a contrary position merely to draw you out and to see if you are willing and able to defend your point of view. Do not start a debate, yet do not surrender a good position. If a position is worth taking, it is worth defending.

14) Do not be afraid to admit an error in judgment if you are shown to be wrong

The board knows that you are forced to reply without any opportunity for careful consideration. Your answer may be demonstrably wrong. If so, admit it and get on with the interview.

15) Do not dwell at length on your present job

The opening question may relate to your present assignment. Answer the question but do not go into an extended discussion. You are being examined for a *new* job, not your present one. As a matter of fact, try to phrase ALL your answers in terms of the job for which you are being examined.

Basis of Rating

Probably you will forget most of these "do's" and "don'ts" when you walk into the oral interview room. Even remembering them all will not ensure you a passing grade. Perhaps you did not have the qualifications in the first place. But remembering them will help you to put your best foot forward, without treading on the toes of the board members.

Rumor and popular opinion to the contrary notwithstanding, an oral board wants you to make the best appearance possible. They know you are under pressure – but they also want to see how you respond to it as a guide to what your reaction would be under the pressures of the job you seek. They will be influenced by the degree of poise you display, the personal traits you show and the manner in which you respond.

ABOUT THIS BOOK

This book contains tests divided into Examination Sections. Go through each test, answering every question in the margin. We have also attached a sample answer sheet at the back of the book that can be removed and used. At the end of each test look at the answer key and check your answers. On the ones you got wrong, look at the right answer choice and learn. Do not fill in the answers first. Do not memorize the questions and answers, but understand the answer and principles involved. On your test, the questions will likely be different from the samples. Questions are changed and new ones added. If you understand these past questions you should have success with any changes that arise. Tests may consist of several types of questions. We have additional books on each subject should more study be advisable or necessary for you. Finally, the more you study, the better prepared you will be. This book is intended to be the last thing you study before you walk into the examination room. Prior study of relevant texts is also recommended. NLC publishes some of these in our Fundamental Series. Knowledge and good sense are important factors in passing your exam. Good luck also helps. So now study this Passbook, absorb the material contained within and take that knowledge into the examination. Then do your best to pass that exam.

EXAMINATION SECTION

EXAMINATION SECTION

TEST 1

DIRECTIONS: Each question or incomplete statement is followed by several suggested answers or completions. Select the one that BEST answers the question or completes the statement. *PRINT THE LETTER OF THE CORRECT ANSWER IN THE SPACE AT THE RIGHT.*

1. The one of the following that is MOST advisable to do before transcribing your dictation notes is to
   A. check the syllabification of long words for typing purposes
   B. edit your notes
   C. number the pages of dictation
   D. sort them by the kind of typing format required

   1._____

2. As a secretary, the one of the following which is LEAST important in writing a letter under your own signature is
   A. the accuracy of the information
   B. the appropriateness of the language
   C. the reason for the letter
   D. your supervisor's approval of the final copy

   2._____

3. In a typed letter, the reference line is used
   A. for identification purposes on typed pages of more than one page
   B. to indicate under what heading the copy of the letter should be filed
   C. to indicate who dictated the letter and who typed it
   D. to make the subject of the letter prominent by typing it a single space below the salutation

   3._____

Questions 4-5:

DIRECTIONS: For questions 4 and 5, choose the letter of the sentence that BEST and MOST clearly expresses its meaning.

4.
   A. It has always been the practice of this office to effectuate recruitment of prospective employees from other departments.
   B. This office has always made a practice of recruiting prospective employees from other departments.
   C. Recruitment of prospective employees from other departments has always been a practice which has been implemented by this office.
   D. Implementation of the policy of recruitment of prospective employees from other departments has always been a practice of this office.

   4._____

5.
   A. These employees are assigned to the level of work evidenced by their efforts and skills during the training period.
   B. The level of work to which these employees is assigned is decided upon on the basis of the efforts and skills evidenced by them during the period in which they were trained.
   C. Assignment of these employees is made on the basis of the level of work their efforts and skills during the training period has evidenced.
   D. These employees are assigned to a level of work their efforts and skills during the training period have evidenced.

5._____

6. An office assistant was asked to mail a duplicated report of 100 pages to a professor in an out-of-town university. The professor sending the report dictated a short letter that he wanted to mail with the report.
Of the following, the MOST inexpensive proper means of sending these two items would be to send the report
   A. and the letter first class
   B. by parcel post and the letter separately by air mail
   C. and the letter by parcel post
   D. by parcel post and attach to the package an envelope with first-class postage in which is enclosed the letter

6._____

7. Plans are underway to determine the productivity of the typists who work in a central office. Of the procedures listed, the one generally considered the MOST accurate for finding out the typists' output is to
   A. keep a record of how much typing is done over specified periods of time
   B. ask each typist how fast she types when she is doing a great deal of word processing
   C. give each typist a timed test during a specified period
   D. ask the supervisor to estimate the typing speed of each subordinate

7._____

8. Assume that an executive regularly receives the four types of mail listed below.
As a general rule, the executive's secretary should arrange the mail from top to bottom so that the top items are
   A. advertisements
   B. airmail letters
   C. business letters
   D. unopened personal letters

8._____

9. An office assistant in transcribing reports and letters from dictation should MOST generally assume that
    A. the transcript should be exactly what was dictated so there is little need to check any details
    B. the dictated material is merely an idea of what the dictator wanted to say so changes should be made to improve any part of the dictation
    C. there may be some slight changes, but essentially the transcription is to be a faithful copy of what was dictated
    D. the transcript is merely a very rough draft and should be typed quickly so that the dictator can review it and make changes preliminary to having the final copy typed

9._____

10. The one of the following which generally is the CHIEF disadvantage of using office machines in place of human workers in office work is that the machines are
    A. slower
    B. less accurate
    C. more costly
    D. less flexible

10._____

11. An office assistant in a New York City college is asked to place a call to a prospective visiting professor in Los Angeles. It is 1 p.m. in New York (EST). The time in Los Angeles is
    A. 9 a.m.   B. 10 a.m.   C. 4 p.m.   D. 5 p.m.

11._____

12. An office assistant is instructed to send a copy of a report to a professor located in a building across campus. The fastest and most efficient way for this report to reach the professor is by
    A. sending a messenger to hand-deliver it to the professor's office
    B. sending it via fax to the main office of the professor's department
    C. e-mailing it to the professor
    D. dictating the contents of the report to the professor over the phone

12._____

13. An office assistant is in the process of typing the forms for recommendation for promotion for a member of the faculty who is away for a week. She notes that two books of which he is the author are listed without dates.
Of the following, the procedure she should BEST follow at this point generally is to
    A. postpone doing the job until the professor returns to campus the following week
    B. type the material omitting the books
    C. check the professor's office for copies of the books and obtain the correct data
    D. call the professor's wife and ask her when the books were published

13._____

14. An office has introduced work standards for all of the employees. Of the following, it is MOST likely that use of such standards would tend to
    A. make it more difficult to determine numbers of employees needed
    B. lead to a substantial drop in morale among all of the employees
    C. reduce the possibility of planning to meet emergencies
    D. reduce uncertainty about the costs of doing tasks

14._____

15. Of the following clerical errors, the one which probably is LEAST important is
    A. adding 543 instead of 548 to a bookkeeping account
    B. putting the wrong code on a data processing card
    C. recording a transaction on the record of Henry Smith instead of on the record of Harry Smith
    D. writing John Murpfy instead of John Murphy when addressing an envelope

15._____

16. Of the following errors, the one which probably is MOST important is
    A. writing "they're" instead of "their" in an office memo
    B. misplacing a decimal point on a sales invoice
    C. forgetting to write the date on a note for a supervisor
    D. sending an e-mail to a misspelled e-mail address

16._____

17. The chairman of an academic department tells an office assistant that a meeting of the faculty is to be held four weeks from the current date. Of the following responsibilities, the office assistant is MOST frequently held responsible for
    A. planning the agenda of the meeting
    B. presiding over the conduct of the meeting
    C. reserving the meeting room and notifying the members
    D. initiating all formal resolutions

17._____

18. Of the following, a centralized filing system is LEAST suitable for filing
    A. material which is confidential in nature
    B. routine correspondence
    C. periodic reports of the divisions of the department
    D. material used by several divisions of the department

18._____

19. A misplaced record is a lost record. Of the following, the MOST valid implication of this statement in regard to office work is that
    A. all records in an office should be filed in strict alphabetical order
    B. accuracy in filing is essential
    C. only one method of filing should be used throughout the office
    D. files should be locked when not in use

19._____

20. When typing names or titles on a roll of folder labels, the one of the following which is MOST important to do is to type the caption   20._____
    A. as it appears on the papers to be placed in the folder
    B. in capital letters
    C. in exact indexing or filing order
    D. so that it appears near the bottom of the folder tab when the label is attached

21. A professor at a Boston university asks an office assistant to place a call to a fellow professor in San Francisco. The MOST appropriate local time for the assistant to place the call to the professor in California, given the time difference, would be   21._____
    A. 8:30 a.m.   B. 10:00 a.m.   C. 11:30 a.m.   D. 1:30 p.m.

22. When typing the rough draft of a report, the computer application you would use is   22._____
    A. Excel   B. Word
    C. PowerPoint   D. Internet Explorer

23. Which of the following is the BEST and most appropriate way to proofread and edit a report before submitting it to a supervisor for review?   23._____
    A. Scan the report with the program's spell check feature
    B. Proof the report yourself, then ask another office assistant to read the report over as well until it is finished
    C. Give the report to another office assistant who is more skilled at proofreading
    D. Use the spell checker, then scan the report yourself as many times as needed in order to pick up any additional errors

24. The one of the following situations in which it would be MOST justifiable for an office to use standard or form paragraphs in its business letters is when   24._____
    A. a large number of similar letters is to be sent
    B. the letters are to be uniform in length and appearance
    C. it is desired to reduce typing errors in correspondence
    D. the office is to carry on a lengthy correspondence with an individual

25. Of the following, the MOST important factor in determining whether or not an office filing system is effective is that the   25._____
    A. information in the files is legible
    B. records in the files are used frequently
    C. information in the files is accurate
    D. records in the files can be located readily

KEY (CORRECT ANSWERS)

1. B	11. B	21. D
2. D	12. C	22. B
3. C	13. C	23. D
4. B	14. D	24. A
5. A	15. D	25. D
6. D	16. B	
7. A	17. C	
8. D	18. A	
9. C	19. B	
10. D	20. C	

TEST 2

DIRECTIONS: Each question or incomplete statement is followed by several suggested answers or completions. Select the one that BEST answers the question or completes the statement. *PRINT THE LETTER OF THE CORRECT ANSWER IN THE SPACE AT THE RIGHT.*

1. For the office assistant whose duties include frequent recording and transcription of minutes of formal meetings, the one of the following reference works generally considered to be MOST useful is
    A. *Robert's Rules of Order*
    B. *Bartlett's Familiar Quotations*
    C. *World Almanac and Book of Facts*
    D. *Conway's Reference*

    1._____

2. Of the following statements about the numeric system of filing, the one which is CORRECT is that it
    A. is the least accurate of all methods of filing
    B. eliminates the need for cross-referencing
    C. allows for very limited expansion
    D. requires a separate index

    2._____

3. When more than one name or subject is involved in a piece of correspondence to be filed, the office assistant should GENERALLY
    A. prepare a cross-reference sheet
    B. establish a geographical filing system
    C. prepare out-guides
    D. establish a separate index card file for noting such correspondence

    3._____

4. A tickler file is MOST generally used for
    A. identification of material contained in a numeric file
    B. maintenance of a current listing of telephone numbers
    C. follow-up of matters requiring future attention
    D. control of records borrowed or otherwise removed from the files

    4._____

5. In filing, the name Ms. *Ann Catalana-Moss* should GENERALLY be indexed as
    A. Moss, Catalana, Ann (Ms.)
    B. Catalana-Moss, Ann (Ms.)
    C. Ann Catalana-Moss (Ms.)
    D. Moss-Catalana, Ann (Ms.)

    5._____

6. An office assistant has a set of four cards, each of which contains one of the following names.
   In alphabetic filing, the FIRST of the cards to be filed is
   A. Ms. Alma John
   B. Mrs. John (Patricia) Edwards
   C. John-Edward School Supplies, Inc.
   D. John H. Edwards

6._____

7. Generally, of the following, the name to be filed FIRST in an alphabetical filing system is
   A. Diane Maestro
   B. Diana McElroy
   C. James Mackell
   D. James McKell

7._____

8. After checking several times, you are unable to locate a student record in its proper file drawer. The file drawer in question is used constantly by many members of the staff.
   In this situation, the NEXT step you should take in locating the missing record is to
   A. ask another worker to look through the file drawer
   B. determine if there is another copy of the record filed in a different place
   C. find out if the record has been removed by another staff member
   D. wait a day or two and see if the record turns up

8._____

9. It is MOST important that an enclosure which is to be mailed with a letter should be put in an envelope so that
   A. any printing on the enclosure will not be visible through the address side of the envelope
   B. it is obvious that there is an enclosure inside the envelope
   C. the enclosure takes up less space than the letter
   D. the person who opens the envelope will pull out both the letter and the enclosure

9._____

10. Suppose that one of the student aides with whom you work suggests a change in the filing procedure. He is sure the change will result in increased rates of filing among the other employees.
    The one of the following which you should do FIRST is to
    A. ask him to demonstrate his method in order to determine if he files more quickly than the other employees
    B. ask your supervisor if you may make a change in the filing procedure
    C. ignore the aide's suggestion since he is not a filing expert
    D. tell him to show his method to the other employees and to encourage them to use it

10._____

11. It is generally advisable to leave at least six inches of working space in a file drawer. This procedure is MOST useful in
    A. decreasing the number of filing errors
    B. facilitating the sorting of documents and folders
    C. maintaining a regular program of removing inactive records
    D. preventing folders and papers from being torn

11._____

12. Assume that a dictator is briefly interrupted because of a telephone call or other similar matter (no more than three minutes).
    Of the following tasks, the person taking the dictation should NORMALLY use the time to
    A. re-read notes already recorded
    B. tidy the dictator's desk
    C. check the accuracy of the dictator's desk files
    D. return to her own desk to type the dictated material

12._____

13. When typing a preliminary draft of a report, the one of the following which you should generally NOT do is
    A. erase typing errors and deletions rather than cross them out
    B. leave plenty of room at the top, bottom and sides of each page
    C. make only the number of copies that you are asked to make
    D. type double or triple space

13._____

14. The BEST way for a receptionist to deal with a situation in which she must leave her desk for a long time is to
    A. ask someone to take her place while she is away
    B. leave a note or sign on her desk which indicates the time she will return
    C. take a chance that no one will arrive while she is gone and leave her desk unattended
    D. tell a coworker to ask any visitors that arrive to wait until she returns

14._____

15. Suppose that two individuals come up to your desk at the same time. One of them asks you for the location of the nearest public phone. After you answer the question, you turn to the second person who asks you the same question.
    The one of the following actions that would be BEST for you to take in this situation is to
    A. ignore the second person since he obviously overheard your first answer
    B. point out that you just answered the same question and quickly repeat the information
    C. politely repeat the information to the second individual
    D. tell the second person to follow the first to the public telephone

15._____

16. Which of the following names should be filed FIRST in an alphabetical filing system?
    A. Anthony Aarvedsen
    B. William Aaron
    C. Denise Aron
    D. A.J. Arrington

17. New material added to a file folder should USUALLY be inserted
    A. in the order of importance (the most important in front)
    B. in the order of importance (the most important in back)
    C. chronologically (most recent in front)
    D. chronologically (most recent in back)

18. An individual is looking for a name in the White Pages of a telephone directory.
    Which of the following BEST describes the system of filing found there?
    A. alphabetic
    B. sequential
    C. locator
    D. index

19. The MAIN purpose of a tickler file is to
    A. help prevent overlooking matters that require future attention
    B. check on adequacy of past performance
    C. pinpoint responsibility for recurring daily tasks
    D. reduce the volume of material kept in general files

20. Which of the following BEST describes the process of *reconciling* a bank statement?
    A. Analyzing the nature of the expenditures made by the office during the preceding month
    B. Comparing the statement of the bank with the banking records maintained in the office
    C. Determining the liquidity position by reading the bank statement carefully
    D. Checking the service charges noted on the bank statement

21. From the viewpoint of preserving agency or institutional funds, the LEAST acceptable method for making a payment is a check made out to
    A. cash
    B. a company
    C. an individual
    D. a partnership

22. Listed below are four of the steps in the process of preparing correspondence for filing.
    If they were to be put in logical sequence, the SECOND step would be
    A. preparing cross-reference sheets or cards
    B. coding the correspondence using a classification system
    C. sorting the correspondence in the order to be filed
    D. checking for follow-up action required and preparing a follow-up slip

23. The process of *justifying* typed copy involves laying out the copy so that 23._____
    A. each paragraph appears to be approximately the same size
    B. no long words are broken up at the end of a line
    C. the right and left hand margins are even
    D. there is enough room to enter proofreading marks at the end of each line

24. The MOST important reason for a person in charge of a petty cash fund 24._____
    to obtain receipts for payments is that this practice would tend to
    A. decrease robberies by delivery personnel
    B. eliminate the need to keep a record of petty cash expenditures
    C. prove that the fund has been used properly
    D. provide a record of the need for cash in the daily operations of the office

25. You should GENERALLY replenish a petty cash fund 25._____
    A. at regularly established intervals
    B. each time you withdraw a sum
    C. when the amount of cash gets below a certain specified amount
    D. when the fund is completely empty

KEY (CORRECT ANSWERS)

1. A	11. D	21. A
2. D	12. A	22. A
3. A	13. A	23. C
4. C	14. A	24. C
5. B	15. C	25. C
6. D	16. B	
7. C	17. C	
8. C	18. A	
9. D	19. A	
10. A	20. B	

EXAMINATION SECTION
TEST 1

DIRECTIONS: Each question or incomplete statement is followed by several suggested answers or completions. Select the one that BEST answers the question or completes the statement. *PRINT THE LETTER OF THE CORRECT ANSWER IN THE SPACE AT THE RIGHT.*

1. If you open a personal letter by mistake, the one of the following actions which it would generally be BEST for you to take is to

    A. ignore your error, attach the envelope to the letter, and distribute in the usual manner
    B. personally give the addressee the letter without any explanation
    C. place the letter inside the envelope, indicate under your initials that it was opened in error, and give to the addressee
    D. reseal the envelope or place the contents in another envelope and pass on to addressee

2. If you receive a telephone call regarding a matter which your office does not handle, you should FIRST

    A. give the caller the telephone number of the proper office so that he can dial again
    B. offer to transfer the caller to the proper office
    C. suggest that the caller re-dial since he probably dialed incorrectly
    D. tell the caller he has reached the wrong office and then hang up

3. When you answer the telephone, the MOST important reason for identifying yourself and your organization is to

    A. give the caller time to collect his or her thoughts
    B. impress the caller with your courtesy
    C. inform the caller that he or she has reached the right number
    D. set a business-like tone at the beginning of the conversation

4. The one of the following cases in which you would NOT place a special notation in the left margin of a letter that you have typed is when

    A. one of the copies is intended for someone other than the addressee of the letter
    B. you enclose a flyer with the letter
    C. you sign your superior's name to the letter, at his or her request
    D. the letter refers to something being sent under separate cover

5. Suppose that you accidentally cut a letter or enclosure as you are opening an envelope with a paper knife.
   The one of the following that you should do FIRST is to

    A. determine whether the document is important
    B. clip or staple the pieces together and process as usual
    C. mend the cut document with transparent tape
    D. notify the sender that the communication was damaged and request another copy

13

2 (#1)

6. As soon as you pick up the phone, a very angry caller begins immediately to complain about city agencies and *red tape*. He says that he has been shifted to two or three different offices. It turns out that he is seeking information which is not immediately available to you. You believe you know, however, where it can be found.
Which of the following actions is the BEST one for you to take?

   A. To eliminate all confusion, suggest that the caller write the mayor stating explicitly what he wants.
   B. Apologize by telling the caller how busy city agencies now are, but also tell him directly that you do not have the information he needs.
   C. Ask for the caller's telephone number, and assure him you will call back after you have checked further.
   D. Give the caller the name and telephone number of the person who might be able to help, but explain that you are not positive he will get results.

6.___

7. Suppose that one of your duties is to dictate responses to routine requests from the public for information. A letter writer asks for information which, as expressed in a one-sentence, explicit agency rule, cannot be given out to the public.
Of the following ways of answering the letter, which is the MOST efficient?

   A. Quote verbatim that section of the agency rules which prohibits giving this information to the public.
   B. Without quoting the rule, explain why you cannot accede to the request and suggest alternative sources.
   C. Describe how carefully the request was considered before classifying it as subject to the rule forbidding the issuance of such information.
   D. Acknowledge receipt of the letter and advise that the requested information is not released to the public.

7.___

8. Suppose you assist in supervising a staff which has rather high morale, and your own supervisor asks you to poll the staff to find out who will be able to work overtime this particular evening to help complete emergency work.
Which of the following approaches would be MOST likely to win their cooperation while maintaining their morale?

   A. Tell them that the better assignments will be given only to those who work overtime.
   B. Tell them that occasional overtime is a job requirement.
   C. Assure them they'll be doing you a personal favor.
   D. Let them know clearly why the overtime is needed.

8.___

9. Suppose that you have been asked to write and to prepare for reproduction new departmental vacation leave regulations.
After you have written the new regulations, all of which fit on two pages, which one of the following would be the BEST method of reproducing 1,000 copies?

   A. An outside private printer because you can best maintain confidentiality using this technique
   B. Photocopying because the copies will have the best possible appearance
   C. Sending the file to all department employees as printable PDFs
   D. Printing and collating on the office high-volume printer

9.___

10. You are in charge of verifying employees' qualifications. This involves telephoning previous employers and schools. One of the applications which you are reviewing contains information which you are almost certain is correct on the basis of what the employee has told you.
    The BEST thing to do is to

    A. check the information again with the employer
    B. perform the required verification procedures
    C. accept the information as valid
    D. ask a superior to verify the information

11. The practice of immediately identifying oneself and one's place of employment when contacting persons on the telephone is

    A. *good* because the receiver of the call can quickly identify the caller and establish a frame of reference
    B. *good* because it helps to set the caller at ease with the other party
    C. *poor* because it is not necessary to divulge that information when making general calls
    D. *poor* because it takes longer to arrive at the topic to be discussed

12. Which one of the following should be the MOST important overall consideration when preparing a recommendation to automate a large-scale office activity?
    The

    A. number of models of automated equipment available
    B. benefits and costs of automation
    C. fears and resistance of affected employees
    D. experience of offices which have automated similar activities

13. A tickler file is MOST appropriate for filing materials

    A. chronologically according to date they were received
    B. alphabetically by name
    C. alphabetically by subject
    D. chronologically according to date they should be followed up

14. Which of the following is the BEST reason for decentralizing rather then centralizing the use of duplicating machines?

    A. Developing and retaining efficient duplicating machine operators
    B. Facilitating supervision of duplicating services
    C. Motivating employees to produce legible duplicated copies
    D. Placing the duplicating machines where they are most convenient and most frequently used

15. Window envelopes are sometimes considered preferable to individually addressed envelopes PRIMARILY because

    A. window envelopes are available in standard sizes for all purposes
    B. window envelopes are more attractive and official-looking
    C. the use of window envelopes eliminates the risk of inserting a letter in the wrong envelope
    D. the use of window envelopes requires neater typing

4 (#1)

16. In planning the layout of a new office, the utilization of space and the arrangement of staff, furnishings, and equipment should usually be MOST influenced by the

    A. gross square footage
    B. status differences in the chain of command
    C. framework of informal relationships among employees
    D. activities to be performed

17. Office forms sometimes consist of several copies, each of a different color. The MAIN reason for using different colors is to

    A. make a favorable impression on the users of the form
    B. distinguish each copy from the others
    C. facilitate the preparation of legible carbon copies
    D. reduce cost, since using colored stock permits recycling of paper

18. Which of the following is the BEST justification for obtaining a photocopying machine for the office?

    A. A photocopying machine can produce an unlimited number of copies at a low fixed cost per copy.
    B. Employees need little training in operating a photocopying machine.
    C. Office costs will be reduced and efficiency increased.
    D. The legibility of a photocopy generally is superior to copy produced by any other office duplicating device.

19. An administrative officer in charge of a small fund for buying office supplies has just written a check to Charles Laird, a supplier, and has sent the check by messenger to him. A half-hour later, the messenger telephones the administrative officer. He has lost the check.
    Which of the following is the MOST important action for the administrative officer to take under these circumstances?

    A. Ask the messenger to return and write a report describing the loss of the check.
    B. Make a note on the performance record of the messenger who lost the check.
    C. Take the necessary steps to have payment stopped on the check.
    D. Refrain from doing anything since the check may be found shortly.

20. A petty cash fund is set up PRIMARILY to

    A. take care of small investments that must be made from time to time
    B. take care of small expenses that arise from time to time
    C. provide a fund to be used as the office wants to use it with little need to maintain records
    D. take care of expenses that develop during emergencies such as machine breakdowns and fires

21. Your superior has asked you to send a package from your agency to a government agency in another city. He has written out the message and has indicated the name of the government agency.
    When you prepare the package for mailing, which of the following items that your superior has not mentioned must you be sure to include?

A. Today's date
B. The full address of the government agency
C. A polite opening such as *Dear Sirs*
D. A final sentence such as *We would appreciate hearing from your agency in reply as soon as is convenient for you*

22. In addition to the original piece of correspondence, one should USUALLY also have typed

    A. a single copy
    B. as many copies as can be typed at one time
    C. no more copies than are needed
    D. two copies

22.____

23. The one of the following which is the BEST procedure to follow when making a short insert in a completed dictation is to

    A. label the insert with a letter and indicate the position of the insert in the text by writing the identifying letter in the proper place
    B. squeeze the insert into its proper place within the main text of the dictation
    C. take down the insert and check the placement with the person who dictated when you are ready to transcribe your notes
    D. transcribe the dictation into longhand, including the insert in its proper position

23.____

24. The one of the following procedures which will be MOST efficient in helping you to quickly open your dictation notebook to a clean sheet is to

    A. clip or place a rubberband around the used portion of the notebook
    B. leave the book out and open to a clean page when not in use
    C. transcribe each dictation after it is given and rip out the used pages
    D. use a book marker to indicate which portion of the notebook has been used

24.____

25. The purpose of dating your dictation notebooks is GENERALLY to

    A. enable you to easily refer to your notes at a later date
    B. ensure that you transcribe your notes in the order in which they were dictated
    C. set up a precise record-keeping procedure
    D. show your employer that you pay attention to detail

25.____

KEY (CORRECT ANSWERS)

1. C
2. B
3. C
4. C
5. C

6. C
7. A
8. D
9. D
10. B

11. A
12. B
13. D
14. D
15. C

16. D
17. B
18. C
19. C
20. B

21. B
22. C
23. A
24. A
25. A

TEST 2

DIRECTIONS: Each question or incomplete statement is followed by several suggested answers or completions. Select the one that BEST answers the question or completes the statement. *PRINT THE LETTER OF THE CORRECT ANSWER IN THE SPACE AT THE RIGHT.*

1. With regard to typed correspondence received by most offices, which of the following is the GREATEST problem?

    A. Verbosity
    B. Illegibility
    C. Improper folding
    D. Excessive copies

2. Of the following, the GREATEST advantage of flash drives over rewritable CD storage is that they

    A. are portable
    B. are both smaller and lighter
    C. contain more storage space
    D. allow files to be deleted to free space

3. Suppose that a large quantity of information is in the files which are located a good distance from your desk. Almost every worker in your office must use these files constantly. Your duties in particular require that you daily refer to about 25 of the same items. They are short, one-page items distributed throughout the files. In this situation, your BEST course would be to

    A. take the items that you use daily from the files and keep them on your desk, inserting *out cards* in their place
    B. go to the files each time you need the information so that the items will be there when other workers need them
    C. make xerox copies of the information you use most frequently and keep them in your desk for ready reference
    D. label the items you use most often with different colored tabs for immediate identification

4. Of the following, the MOST important advantage of preparing manuals of office procedures in loose-leaf form is that this form

    A. permits several employees to use different sections simultaneously
    B. facilitates the addition of new material and the removal of obsolete material
    C. is more readily arranged in alphabetical order
    D. reduces the need for cross-references to locate material carried under several headings

5. Suppose that you establish a new clerical procedure for the unit you supervise. Your keeping a close check on the time required by your staff to handle the new procedure is WISE mainly because such a check will find out

    A. whether your subordinates know how to handle the new procedure
    B. whether a revision of the unit's work schedule will be necessary as a result of the new procedure
    C. what attitude your employees have toward the new procedure
    D. what alterations in job descriptions will be necessitated by the new procedure

6. The numbered statements below relate to the stenographic skill of taking dictation. According to authorities on secretarial practices, which of these are generally recommended guides to development of efficient stenographic skills?

   STATEMENTS
   1. A stenographer should date her notebook daily to facilitate locating certain notes at a later time.
   2. A stenographer should make corrections of grammatical mistakes while her boss is dictating to her.
   3. A stenographer should draw a line through the dictated matter in her notebook after she has transcribed it.
   4. A stenographer should write in longhand unfamiliar names and addresses dictated to her.

   The CORRECT answer is:

   A. Only Statements 1, 2, and 3 are generally recommended guides.
   B. Only Statements 2, 3, and 4 are generally recommended guides.
   C. Only Statements 1, 3, and 4 are generally recommended guides.
   D. All four statements are generally recommended guides.

7. According to generally recognized rules of filing in an alphabetic filing system, the one of the following names which normally should be filed LAST is

   A. Department of Education, New York State
   B. F.B.I.
   C. Police Department of New York City
   D. P.S. 81 of New York City

8. Which one of the following forms for the typed name of the dictator in the closing lines of a letter is generally MOST acceptable in the United States?

   A. (Dr.) James F. Fenton
   B. Dr. James F. Fenton
   C. Mr. James F. Fenton, Ph.D.
   D. James F. Fenton

9. Which of the following is, MOST generally, a rule to be followed when typing a rough draft?

   A. The copy should be single spaced.
   B. The copy should be triple spaced.
   C. There is no need for including footnotes.
   D. Errors must be neatly corrected.

10. An office assistant needs a synonym.
    Of the following, the book which she would find MOST useful is

    A. a world atlas
    B. BARTLETT'S FAMILIAR QUOTATIONS
    C. a manual of style
    D. a thesaurus

11. Of the following examples of footnotes, the one that is expressed in the MOST generally accepted standard form is:

    A. Johnson, T.F. (Dr.), <u>English for Everyone</u>, 3rd or 4th edition; New York City Linton Publishing Company, p. 467
    B. Frank Taylor, <u>English for Today</u> (New York: Rayton Publishing Company, 1971), p. 156
    C. Ralph Wilden, <u>English for Tomorrow,</u> Reynolds Publishing Company, England, p. 451
    D. Quinn, David, Yesterday's English (New York: Baldwin Publishing Company, 1972), p. 431

12. Standard procedures are used in offices PRIMARILY because

    A. an office is a happier place if everyone is doing the tasks in the same manner
    B. particular ways of doing jobs are considered more efficient than other ways
    C. it is good discipline for workers to follow standard procedures approved by the supervisor
    D. supervisors generally don't want workers to be creative in planning their work

13. Assume that an office assistant has the responsibility for compiling, typing, and mailing a preliminary announcement of Spring term course offerings. The announcement will go to approximately 900 currently enrolled students. Assuming that the following equipment is available for use, the MOST EFFECTIVE method for distributing the announcement to all 900 students is to

    A. e-mail it as a text document using the electronic student mailing list
    B. post the announcement as a PDF document for download on the department website
    C. send it by fax
    D. post the announcement and leave copies in buildings around campus

14. *Justified typing* is a term that refers MOST specifically to typewriting copy

    A. that has been edited and for which final copy is being prepared
    B. in a form that allows for an even right-hand margin
    C. with a predetermined vertical placement for each alternate line
    D. that has been approved by the supervisor and his superior

15. Which one of the following is the BEST form for the address in a letter?

    A. Mr. John Jones
       Vice President, The Universal Printing Company
       1220 Fifth Avenue
       New York, 10023 New York
    B. Mr. John Jones, Vice President
       The Universal Printing Company
       1220 Fifth Avenue
       New York, New York 10023
    C. Mr. John Jones, Vice President, The Universal Printing Company
       1220 Fifth Avenue
       New York, New York 10023

D. Mr. John Jones Vice President,
The Universal Printing Company
1220 Fifth Avenue
New York, 10023 New York

16. Of the following, the CHIEF advantage of the use of window envelopes over ordinary envelopes is that window envelopes

    A. eliminate the need for addressing envelopes
    B. protect the confidential nature of enclosed material
    C. cost less to buy than ordinary envelopes
    D. reduce the danger of the address becoming illegible

17. In the complimentary close of a business letter, the FIRST letter of _____ should be capitalized.

    A. all the words
    B. none of the words
    C. only the first word
    D. only the last word

18. Assume that one of your duties is to procure needed office supplies from the supply room. You are permitted to draw supplies every two weeks.
    The one of the following which would be the MOST desirable practice for you to follow in obtaining supplies is to

    A. obtain a quantity of supplies sufficient to last for several months to make certain that enough supplies are always on hand
    B. determine the minimum supply necessary to keep on hand for the various items and obtain an additional quantity as soon as possible after the supply on hand has been reduced to this minimum
    C. review the supplies once a month to determine what items have been exhausted and obtain an additional quantity as soon as possible
    D. obtain a supply of an item as soon after it has been exhausted as is possible

19. Some offices that keep carbon copies of letters use several different colors of carbon paper for making carbon copies.
    Of the following, the CHIEF reason for using different colors of carbon paper is to

    A. facilitate identification of different types of letters in the files
    B. relieve the monotony of typing and filing carbon copies
    C. reduce the costs of preparing carbon copies
    D. utilize both sides of the carbon paper for typing

20. Your supervisor asks you to post an online ad for freelance designers interested in submitting samples for a new company logo. Prospective workers should be proficient in which of the following software?

    A. Microsoft Word
    B. Adobe Acrobat Pro
    C. Adobe Illustrator
    D. Microsoft PowerPoint

21. Gary Thompson is applying for a position with the firm of Gray and Williams.
    Which letter should be filed in top position in the *Application* folder?

    A. A letter of recommendation written on September 18 by Johnson & Smith
    B. Williams' letter of October 8 requesting further details regarding Thompson's experience

C. Thompson's letter of September 8 making application for a position as sales manager
D. Letter of September 20 from Alfred Jackson recommending Thompson for the job

22. The USUAL arrangement in indexing the names of the First National Bank, Toledo, is

   A. First National Bank, Toledo, Ohio
   B. Ohio, First National Bank, Toledo
   C. Toledo, First National Bank, Ohio
   D. Ohio, Toledo, First National Bank

23. A single line through typed text indicating that it's incorrect or invalid is known as a(n)

   A. underline
   B. strikethrough
   C. line font
   D. eraser

24. A typical e-mail with an attachment should contain all of the following for successful transmittal EXCEPT

   A. recipient's address   B. file attachment
   C. body text   D. description of attachment

25. The subject line in a letter is USUALLY typed a _____ space below the _____.

   A. single; inside address   B. single; salutation
   C. double; inside address   D. double; salutation

KEY (CORRECT ANSWERS)

1.	A	11.	B
2.	C	12.	B
3.	C	13.	A
4.	B	14.	B
5.	B	15.	B
6.	C	16.	A
7.	D	17.	C
8.	D	18.	B
9.	B	19.	A
10.	D	20.	C

21. B
22. A
23. B
24. D
25. D

EXAMINATION SECTION
TEST 1

DIRECTIONS: Each question or incomplete statement is followed by several suggested answers or completions. Select the one that BEST answers the question or completes the statement. *PRINT THE LETTER OF THE CORRECT ANSWER IN THE SPACE AT THE RIGHT.*

1. Records of one type or another are kept in every office. The MOST important of the following reasons for the supervisor of a clerical or stenographic unit to keep statistical records of the work done in his unit is generally to
   A. supply basic information needed in planning the work of the unit
   B. obtain statistics for comparison with other units
   C. serve as the basis for unsatisfactory employee evaluation
   D. provide the basis for special research projects on program budgeting

   1.____

2. It is better for an employee to report and be responsible directly to several supervisors than to report and be responsible to only one supervisor.
   This statement directly CONTRADICTS the supervisory principle generally known as
   A. span of control
   B. unity of command
   C. delegation of authority
   D. accountability

   2.____

3. The one of the following which would MOST likely lead to friction among clerks in a unit is for the unit supervisor to
   A. defend the actions of his clerks when discussing them with his own supervisor
   B. praise each of his clerks in confidence as the best clerk in the unit
   C. get his men to work together as a team in completing the work of the unit
   D. consider the point of view of the rank and file clerks when assigning unpleasant tasks

   3.____

4. You become aware that one of the employees you supervise has failed to follow correct procedure and has been permitting various reports to be prepared, typed, and transmitted improperly.
   The BEST action for you to take FIRST in this situation is to
   A. order the employee to review all departmental procedures and reprimand him for having violated them
   B. warn the employee that he must obey regulations because uniformity is essential for effective departmental operation
   C. confer with the employee both about his failure to follow regulations and his reasons for doing so
   D. watch the employee's work very closely in the future but say nothing about this violation

   4.____

5. The supervisory clerk who would be MOST likely to have poor control over his subordinates is the one who
   A. goes to unusually great lengths to try to win their approval
   B. pitches in with the work they are doing during periods of heavy workload when no extra help can be obtained
   C. encourages and helps his subordinates toward advancement
   D. considers suggestions from his subordinates before establishing new work procedures involving them

6. Suppose that a clerk who has been transferred to your office from another division in your agency because of difficulties with his supervisor has been placed under your supervision.
   The BEST course of action for you to take FIRST is to
   A. instruct the clerk in the duties he will be performing in your office and make him feel wanted in his new position
   B. analyze the clerk's past grievance to determine if the transfer was the best solution to the problem
   C. advise him of the difficulties his former supervisor had with other employees and encourage him not to feel bad about the transfer
   D. warn him that you will not tolerate any nonsense and that he will be under continuous surveillance while assigned to you

7. A certain office supervisor takes the initiative to represent his employees' interests related to working conditions, opportunities for advancement, etc. to his own supervisor and the administrative levels of the agency.
   This supervisor's actions will MOST probably have the effect of
   A. preventing employees from developing individual initiative in their work goals
   B. encouraging employees to compete openly for the special attention of their supervisor
   C. depriving employees of the opportunity to be represented by persons and/or unions of their own choosing
   D. building employee confidence in their supervisor and a spirit of cooperation in their work

8. Suppose that you have been promoted, assigned as a supervisor of a certain unit, and asked to reorganize its functions so that specific routine procedures can be established.
   Before deciding which routines to establish, the FIRST of the following steps you should take is to
   A. decide who will perform each task in the routine
   B. determine the purpose to be served by each routine procedure
   C. outline the sequence of steps in each routine to be established
   D. calculate if more staff will be needed to carry out the new procedures

9. When routine procedures covering the ordinary work of an office are established, the supervisor of the office tends to be relieved of the need to
   A. make repeated decisions on the handling of recurring similar situations
   B. check the accuracy of the work completed by his subordinates
   C. train his subordinates in new work procedures
   D. plan and schedule the work of his office

9._____

10. Of the following, the method which would be LEAST helpful to a supervisor in effectively applying the principles of on-the-job safety to the daily work of his unit is for him to
    A. initiate corrections of unsafe layouts of equipment and unsafe work processes
    B. take charge of operations that are not routine to make certain that safety precautions are established and observed
    C. continue to talk safety and promote safety consciousness in his subordinates
    D. figure the cost of all accidents which could possibly occur on the job

10._____

11. A clerk is assigned to serve as receptionist for a large and busy office. Although many members of the public visit this office, the clerk often experiences periods of time in which he has nothing to do.
    In these circumstances, the MOST advisable of the following actions for the supervisor to take is to
    A. assign a number of relatively low priority clerical jobs to the receptionist to do in the slow periods
    B. regularly rotate this assignment so that all of the clerks experience this lighter work load
    C. assign the receptionist job as part of the duties of a number of clerks whose desks are nearest the reception room
    D. overlook the situation since most of the receptionist's time is spent in performing a necessary and meaningful function

11._____

12. For a supervisor to require all stenographers in a stenographic pool to produce the same amount of work on a particular day is
    A. advisable since it will prove that the supervisor plays no favorites
    B. fair since all stenographers are receiving approximately the same salary, their output should be equivalent
    C. not necessary since the fast workers will compensate for the slow workers
    D. not realistic since individual differences in abilities and work assignment must be taken into consideration

12._____

13. The establishment of a centralized typing pool to service the various units in an organization is MOST likely to be worthwhile when there is
    A. wide fluctuation from time to time in the needs of the various units for typing service
    B. a large volume of typing work to be done in each of the units
    C. a need by each unit for different kinds of typing service
    D. a training program in operation to develop and maintain typing skills

13._____

4 (#1)

14. A newly appointed supervisor should learn as much as possible about the backgrounds of his subordinates. This statement is GENERALLY correct because
    A. knowing their backgrounds assures they will be treated objectively, equally, and without favor
    B. effective handling of subordinates is based upon knowledge of their individual differences
    C. subordinates perform more efficiently under one supervisor than under another
    D. subordinates have confidence in a supervisor who knows all about them

14.____

15. The use of electronic computers in modern businesses has produced many changes in office and information management.
    Of the following, it would NOT be correct to state that computer utilization
    A. broadens the scope of managerial and supervisory authority
    B. establishes uniformity in the processing and reporting of information
    C. cuts costs by reducing the personnel needed for efficient office operation
    D. supplies management rapidly with up-to-date data to facilitate decision-making

15.____

16. The CHIEF advantage of having a single, large open office instead of small partitioned ones for a clerical unit or stenographic pool is that the single, large open office
    A. afford privacy without isolation for all office workers not directly dealing with the public
    B. assures the smoother, more continuous inter-office flow of work that is essential for efficient work production
    C. facilitates the office supervisor's visual control over and communication with his subordinates
    D. permits a more decorative and functional arrangement of office furniture and machines

16.____

17. When a supervisor provides a new employee with the information necessary for a basic knowledge and a general understanding of practices and procedures of the agency, he is applying the type of training generally known as _____ training.
    A. pre-employment   B. induction
    C. on-the-job   D. supervisory

17.____

18. Many government agencies require the approval by a central forms control unit of the design and reproduction of new office forms.
    The one of the following results of this procedure that is a DISADVANTAGE is that requiring prior approval of a central forms control unit usually
    A. limits the distribution of forms to those offices with justifiable reasons for receiving them
    B. permits checking whether existing forms or modifications of them are in line with current agency needs

18.____

C. encourages reliance on only the central office to set up all additional forms when needed
D. provides for someone with a specialized knowledge of forms design to review and criticize new and revised forms

19. Suppose that a large quantity of information is in the files which are located a good distance from your desk. Almost every worker in your office must use these files constantly. Your duties in particular require that you refer daily to about 25 of the same items. They are short, one-page items distributed throughout the files.
In this situation, your BEST course would be to
    A. take the items that you use daily from the files and keep them on your desk, inserting out cards in their place
    B. go to the files each time you need the information so that the items will be there when other workers need them
    C. make Xerox copies of the information you use most frequently and keep them in your desk for ready reference
    D. label the items you use most often with different colored tabs for immediate identification

20. Of the following, the MOST important advantage of preparing manuals of office procedures in loose-leaf form is that this form
    A. permits several employees to use different sections simultaneously
    B. facilitates the addition of new material and the removal of obsolete material
    C. is more readily arranged in alphabetical order
    D. reduces the need for cross-references to locate material carried under several headings

21. Suppose that you establish a new clerical procedure for the unit you supervise. Your keeping a close check on the time required by your staff to handle the new procedure is WISE mainly because such a check will find out
    A. whether your subordinates know how to handle the new procedure
    B. whether a revision of the unit's work schedule will be necessary as a result of the new procedure
    C. what attitude your employees have toward the new procedure
    D. what alterations in job descriptions will be necessitated by the new procedure

22. From the viewpoint of an office supervisor, the BEST of the following reasons for distributing the incoming mail before the beginning of the regular work day is that
    A. distribution can be handled quickly and most efficiently at that time
    B. distribution later in the day may be distracting to or interfere with other employees
    C. the employees who distribute the mail can then perform other tasks during the rest of the day
    D. office activities for the day based on the mail may then be started promptly

23. Suppose you are the head of a unit with ten staff members who are located in several different rooms.
If you want to inform your staff of a minor change in procedure, the BEST and LEAST expensive way of doing so would usually be to
   A. send a copy to each staff member
   B. call a special staff meeting and announce the change
   C. circulate a memo, having each staff member initial it
   D. have a clerk tell each member of the staff about the change

24. The numbered statements below relate to the stenographic skill of taking dictation. According to authorities on secretarial practices, which of these are generally recommended guides to development of efficient stenographic skills?
   I. A stenographer should date her notebook daily to facilitate locating certain notes at a later time.
   II. A stenographer should make corrections of grammatical mistakes while her boss is dictating to her.
   III. A stenographer should draw a line through the dictated matter in her notebook after she has transcribed it
   IV. A stenographer should write in longhand unfamiliar names and addresses dictated to her.

   The CORRECT answer is:
   A. Only Statements I, II, and III are generally recommended guides.
   B. Only Statements II, III, and IV are generally recommended guides.
   C. Only Statements I, III, and IV are generally recommended guides.
   D. All four statements are generally recommended guides.

25. A bureau of a city agency is about to move to a new location.
Of the following, the FIRST step that should be taken in order to provide a good layout for the office at the new location is to
   A. decide the exact amount of space to be assigned to each unit of the bureau
   B. decide whether to lay out a single large open office or one consisting of small partitioned units
   C. ask each unit chief in the bureau to examine the new location and submit a request for the amount of space he needs
   D. prepare a detailed plan of the dimensions of the floor space to be occupied by the bureau at the new location

26. Of the following, the BEST reason for discarding a sheet of carbon paper is that
   A. some carbon rubs off on your fingers when handled
   B. there are several creases in the sheet
   C. the short edge of the sheet is curled
   D. the finish on the sheet is smooth and shiny

27. Suppose you are the supervisor of a mailroom of a large city agency where the mail received daily is opened by machine, sorted by hand for delivery, and time-stamped. Letters and any enclosures are removed from envelopes and stapled together before distribution. One of your newest clerks asks you what should be done when a letter makes reference to an enclosure but no enclosure is in the envelope.
You should tell him that, in this situation, the BEST procedure is to
    A. make an entry of the sender's name and address in the missing enclosures file and forward the letter to its proper destination
    B. return the letter to its sender, attaching a request for the missing enclosure
    C. put the letter aside until a proper investigation may be made concerning the missing enclosure
    D. route the letter to the person for whom it is intended, noting the absence of the enclosure on the letter-margin

28. The term *work flow*, when used in connection with office management or the activities in an office, GENERALLY means the
    A. use of charts in the analysis of various office functions
    B. rate of speed at which work flows through a single section of an office
    C. step-by-step physical routing of work through its various procedures
    D. number of individual work units which can be produced by the average employee

29. Physical conditions can have a definite effect on the efficiency and morale of an office. Which of the following statements about physical conditions in an office is CORRECT?
    A. Hard, non-porous surfaces reflect more noise than linoleum on the top of a desk.
    B. Painting in tints of bright yellow is more appropriate for sunny, well-lit offices than for dark, poorly-lit offices.
    C. Plate glass is better than linoleum for the top of a desk.
    D. The central typing room needs less light than a conference room does.

30. In a certain filing system, documents are consecutively numbered as they are filed, a register is maintained of such consecutively numbered documents, and a record is kept of the number of each document removed from the files and its destination.
This system will NOT help in
    A. finding the present whereabouts of a particular document
    B. proving the accuracy of the data recorded on a certain document
    C. indicating whether observed existing documents were ever filed
    D. locating a desired document without knowing what its contents are

31. In deciding the kind and number of records an agency should keep, the administrative staff must recognize that records are of value in office management PRIMARILY as
    A. informational bases for agency activities
    B. data for evaluating the effectiveness of the agency
    C. raw material on which statistical analyses are to be based
    D. evidence that the agency is carrying out its duties and responsibilities

32. Complaints are often made by the public about the government's procedures. Although in most cases such procedures cannot be changed since various laws and regulations require them, it may still be possible to reduce the number of complaints.
    Which one of the following actions by personnel dealing with applicants for city services is LEAST likely to reduce complaints concerning city procedures?
    A. Treating all citizens alike and explaining to them that no exceptions to required procedures can be made.
    B. Explaining briefly to the citizen why he should comply with regulations.
    C. Being careful to avoid mistakes which may make additional interviews or correspondence necessary.
    D. Keeping the citizen informed of the progress of his correspondence when immediate disposition cannot be made.

33. Persons whose native language is not English sometimes experience difficulty in communication when visiting public offices.
    The MOST common method used by such persons to overcome the difficulty in communication is to
    A. write in their own language whatever they wish to say
    B. hire a professional interpreter
    C. ask a patrolman for assistance
    D. bring with them an English-speaking friend or relative

34. In answering a complaint made by a member of the public that a certain essential procedure required by your agency is difficult to follow, it would be BEST for you to stress most
    A. that a change in the rules may be considered if enough complaints are received
    B. why the operation of a large agency sometimes proves a hardship in individual cases
    C. the necessity for the procedure
    D. the origin of the procedure

35. When talking to a citizen, it is BEST for an employee of government to
    A. use ordinary conversational phrases and a natural manner
    B. try to copy the pronunciation and level of education shown by the citizen
    C. try to speak in a very cultured manner and tone
    D. use technical terms to show his familiarity with his own work

36. Employees who service the public should maintain an attitude which is both sympathetic and objective. An unsympathetic and subjective attitude would be shown by a public employee who
    A. says *no* with a smile when a citizen's request must be denied
    B. listens attentively to a long complaint from a citizen about government's *red tape*
    C. responds with sarcasm when a citizen asks a question which has an obvious manner
    D. suggests a definite solution to a citizen's problems

37. Of the following methods of conducting an interview, the BEST is to
    A. ask questions with *yes* or *no* answers
    B. listen carefully and ask only questions that are pertinent
    C. fire questions at the interviewee so that he must answer sincerely and briefly
    D. read standardized questions to the person being interviewed

38. An interviewer should begin with topics which are easy to talk about and which are not threatening. This procedure is useful MAINLY because it
    A. allows the applicant a little time to get accustomed to the situation and leads to freer communication
    B. distracts the attention of the person being interviewed from the main purpose of the questioning
    C. is the best way for the interviewer to show that he is relaxed and confident on the job
    D. causes the interviewee to feel that the interviewer is apportioning valuable questioning time

39. The initial interview will normally be more of a problem to the interviewer than any subsequent interviews he may have with the same person because
    A. the interviewee is likely to be hostile
    B. there is too much to be accomplished in one session
    C. he has less information about the client than he will have later
    D. some information may be forgotten when later making record of this first interview

40. You are a supervisor in an agency and are holding your first interview with a new employee. In this interview, you should strive MAINLY to
    A. show the new employee that you are an efficient and objective supervisor, with a completely impersonal attitude toward your subordinate
    B. complete the entire orientation process including the giving of detailed job-duty instructions
    C. make it clear to the employee that all your decisions are based on your many years of experience
    D. lay the groundwork for a good employee-supervisor relationship by gaining the new employee's confidence

41. Most successful interviews are those in which the interviewer shows a genuine interest in the person he is questioning. This attitude would MOST likely cause the individual being interviewed to
    A. feel that the interviewer already knows all the facts in his case
    B. act more naturally and reveal more of his true feelings
    C. request that the interviewer give more attention to his problems, not his personality
    D. react defensively, suppress his negative feelings, and conceal the real facts in his case

42. Questions worded so that the person being interviewed has some hint of the desired answer can modify the person's response. The result of the inclusion of such questions in an interview, even when they are used inadvertently, is to
    A. have no effect on the basic content of the information given by the person interviewed
    B. have value in convincing the person that the suggested plan is the best for him
    C. cause the person to give more meaningful information
    D. reduce the validity of the information obtained from the person

43. The person MOST likely to be a good interviewer is one who
    A. is able to outguess the person being interviewed
    B. tries to change the attitudes of the persons he interviews
    C. controls the interview by skillfully dominating the conversation
    D. is able to imagine himself in the position of the person being interviewed

44. The *halo effect* is an overall impression on the interviewer, whether favorable or unfavorable, usually created by a single trait. This impression then influences the appraisal of all other factors.
    A *halo effect* is LEAST likely to be created at an interview where the interviewee is a
    A. person of average appearance and ability
    B. rough-looking man who uses abusive language
    C. young attractive woman being interviewed by a man
    D. person who demonstrates an exceptional ability to remember facts

45. Of the following, the BEST way for an interviewer to calm a person who seems to have become emotionally upset as a result of a question asked is for the interviewer to
    A. talk to the person about other things for a short time
    B. ask that the person control himself
    C. probe for the cause of his emotional upset
    D. finish the questioning as quickly as possible

46. Of the following, a centralized filing system is LEAST suitable for filing
    A. material which is confidential in nature
    B. routine correspondence
    C. periodic reports of the divisions of the department
    D. material used by several divisions of the department

47. Form letters should be used MAINLY when
    A. an office has to reply to a great many similar inquiries
    B. the type of correspondence varies widely
    C. it is necessary to have letters which are well-phrased and grammatically correct
    D. letters of inquiry have to be answered as soon as possible after they are received

48. Suppose that you are assigned to prepare a form from which certain information will be posted in a ledger. It would be MOST helpful to the person posting the information in the ledger is, in designing the form, you were to
    A. use the same color paper for both the form and the ledger
    B. make the form the same size as the pages of the ledger
    C. have the information on the form in the same order as that used in the ledger
    D. include in the form a box which is to be initialed when the data on the form have been posted in the ledger

49. A misplaced record is a lost record. Of the following, the MOST valid implication of this statement in regard to office work is that
    A. all records in an office should be filed in strict alphabetical order
    B. accuracy in filing is essential
    C. only one method of filing should be used throughout the office
    D. files should be locked when not in use

50. James Jones is applying for a provisional appointment as a clerk in your department. He presents a letter of recommendation from a former employer stating: *James Jones was rarely late or absent; he has a very pleasing manner and never got into an argument with his fellow employees.*
    The above information concerning this applicant
    A. proves clearly that he produces more work than the average employee
    B. indicates that he was probably attempting to conceal his inefficiency from his former employer
    C. presents no conclusive evidence of his ability to do clerical work
    D. indicates clearly that with additional training he will make a good supervisor

KEY (CORRECT ANSWERS)

1. A	11. A	21. B	31. A	41. B
2. B	12. D	22. D	32. A	42. D
3. B	13. A	23. C	33. D	43. D
4. C	14. B	24. C	34. C	44. A
5. A	15. A	25. D	35. A	45. A
6. A	16. C	26. B	36. C	46. A
7. D	17. B	27. D	37. B	47. A
8. B	18. C	28. C	38. A	48. C
9. A	19. C	29. A	39. C	49. B
10. D	20. B	30. B	40. D	50. C

TEST 2

DIRECTIONS: Each question or incomplete statement is followed by several suggested answers or completions. Select the one that BEST answers the question or completes the statement. *PRINT THE LETTER OF THE CORRECT ANSWER IN THE SPACE AT THE RIGHT.*

Questions 1-10.

DIRECTIONS: In each of Questions 1 through 10, there is a quotation which contains a word (one of those underlined) that is either incorrectly used because it is not in keeping with the meaning the quotation is evidently intended to convey, or is misspelled. There is only one incorrect word in each quotation. Of the four underlined words in each question, determine if the first one should be replaced by the word lettered A, the second replaced by the word lettered B, the third replaced by the word lettered C, or the fourth replaced by the word lettered D. Print the letter of the replacement word you have selected in the space at the right.

1. Whether one depends on flourescent or artificial light or both, adequate standards should be maintained by means of systematic tests.
 A. natural B. safeguards C. established D. routine

2. A policeman has to be prepared to assume his knowledge as a social scientist in the community.
 A. forced B. role C. philosopher D. street

3. It is practically impossible to tell whether a sentence is very long simply by measuring its length.
 A. almost B. mark C. too D. denoting

4. By using carbon paper, the typist easily is able to insert as many as six copies of a report.
 A. adding B. seldom C. make D. forms

5. Although all people have many traits in common, a receptionist in her agreements with people learns quickly how different each person is from every other person.
 A. impressions B. associations C. decides D. various

6. Strong leaders are required to organize a community for delinquency prevention and for dissemination of organized crime and drug addiction.
 A. tactics B. important C. control D. meetings

7. The demonstrators, who were taken to the Criminal Courts building in Manhattan (because it was large enough to accommodate them), contended that the arrests were unwarrented.
 A. demonstraters B. Manhatten C. accomodate D. unwarranted

8. When two or more forms for spelling a word exist, it is <u>advisable</u> to use the <u>preferred</u> spelling indicated in the <u>dictionary</u>, and to use it <u>consistantly</u>. 8.____
   A. adviseable   B. prefered   C. dictionery   D. consistently

9. If you know the language of the <u>foreign</u> country you are visiting, your <u>embarassment</u> will <u>disappear</u> and you will learn a lot more about the customs and <u>characteristics</u>. 9.____
   A. foriegn   B. embarrassment
   C. dissappear   D. charactaristics

10. Material consisting of government bulletins, <u>adverticements</u>, <u>catalogues</u>, <u>announcements</u> of address changes and any other <u>periodical</u> material of this nature, may be filed alphabetically according to subject. 10.____
    A. advertisements   B. cataloges
    C. announcments   D. pereodical

Questions 11-14.

DIRECTIONS: Each of the two sentences in Questions 11 through 14 may contain errors in punctuation, capitalization, or grammar.
If there is an error in only Sentence I, mark your answer A.
If there is an error in only Sentence II, mark you answer B.
If there is an error in both Sentences I and II, mark your answer C.
If both Sentences I and II are correct, mark your answer D.

11. I. It is very annoying to have a pencil sharpener, which is not in proper working order. 11.____
    II. The building watchman checked the door of Charlie's office and found that the lock has been jammed.

12. I. Since he went on the New York City council a year ago, one of his primary concerns has been safety in the streets. 12.____
    II. After waiting in the doorway for about 15 minutes, a black sedan appeared.

13. I. When you are studying a good textbook is important. 13.____
    II. He said he would divide the money equally between you and me.

14. I. The question is, "How can a large number of envelopes be sealed rapidly without the use of a sealing machine?" 14.____
    II. The administrator assigned two stenographers, Mary and I, to the new bureau.

Questions 15-16.

DIRECTIONS: In each of Questions 15 and 16, the four sentences are from a paragraph in a report. They are not in the right order. Which of the following arrangements is the BEST one?

15.
I. An executive may answer a letter by writing his reply on the face of the letter itself instead of having a return letter typed.
II. This procedure is efficient because it saves the executive's time, the typist's time, and saves office file space.
III. Copying machines are used in small offices as well as large offices to save time and money in making brief replies to business letters.
IV. A copy is made on a copying machine to go into the company files, while the original is mailed back to the sender.

The CORRECT answer is:
A. I, II, IV, III B. I, IV, II, III C. III, I, IV, II D. III, IV, II, I

16.
I. Most organizations favor one of the types but always include the others to a lesser degree.
II. However, we can detect a definite trend toward greater uses of symbolic control.
III. We suggest that our local police agencies are today primarily utilizing material control.
IV. Control can be classified into three types: physical, material, and symbolic.

The CORRECT answer is:
A. IV, II, III, I B. II, I, IV, III C. III, IV, II, I D. IV, I, III, II

17. Of the following, the MOST effective report writing style is usually characterized by
A. covering all the main ideas in the same paragraph
B. presenting each significant point in a new paragraph
C. placing the least important points before the most important points
D. giving all points equal emphasis throughout the report

18. Of the following, which factor is COMMON to all types of reports?
A. Presentation of information
B. Interpretation of findings
C. Chronological ordering of the information
D. Presentation of conclusions and recommendations

19. When writing a report, the one of the following which you should do FIRST is
A. set up a logical work schedule
B. determine your objectives in writing the report
C. select your statistical material
D. obtain the necessary data from the files

20. Generally, the frequency with which reports are to be submitted or the length of the interval which they cover should depend MAINLY on the
    A. amount of time needed to prepare the reports
    B. degree of comprehensiveness required in the reports
    C. availability of the data to be included in the reports
    D. extent of the variations in the data with the passage of time

21. The objectiveness of a report is its unbiased presentation of the facts.
    If this be so, which of the following reports listed below is likely to be the MOST objective?
    A. The Best Use of an Electronic Computer in Department Z
    B. The Case for Raising the Salaries of Employees in Department A
    C. Quarterly Summary of Production in the Duplicating Unit of Department Y
    D. Recommendation to Terminate Employee X's Services Because of Misconduct

Questions 22-27.

DIRECTIONS: Questions 22 through 27 are to be answered SOLELY on the basis of the information contained in the charts below which relate to the budget allocations of City X, a small suburban community. The charts depict the annual budget allocations by Department and by Expenditures over a five-year period.

CITY X BUDGET IN MILLIONS OF DOLLARS

TABLE I. Budget Allocations By Department					
Department	2012	2013	2014	2015	2016
Public Safety	30	45	50	40	50
Health and Welfare	50	75	90	60	70
Engineering	5	8	10	5	8
Human Resources	10	12	20	10	22
Conversation and Environment	10	15	20	20	15
Education and Development	15	25	35	15	15
TOTAL BUDGET	120	180	225	150	180

TABLE II. Budget Allocations by Expenditures					
Category	2012	2013	2014	2015	2016
Raw Materials and Machinery	36	63	68	30	98
Capital Outlay	12	27	56	15	18
Personal Services	72	90	101	105	65
TOTAL BUDGET	120	180	225	150	180

22. The year in which the SMALLEST percentage of the total annual budget was allocated to the Department of Education and Development is
    A. 2012   B. 2013   C. 2015   D. 2016

5 (#2)

23. Assume that, in 2015, the Department of Conservation and Environment divided its annual budget into the three categories of expenditures and in exactly the same proportion as the budget shown in Table II for the year 2015. The amount allocated for capital outlay in the Department of Conservation and Environment's 2015 budget was MOST NEARLY _____ million.
    A. $2 B. $4 C. $6 D. $10

    23.____

24. From the year 2013 to the year 2015, the sum of the annual budgets for the Departments of Public Safety and Engineering showed an overall _____ of _____ million.
    A. decline; $8   B. increase; $7   C. decline; $15   D. increase; $22

    24.____

25. The LARGEST dollar increase in departmental budget allocations from one year to the next was in
    A. Public Safety from 2012 to 2013
    B. Health and Welfare from 2012 to 2013
    C. Education and Development from 2014 to 2015
    D. Human Resources from 2014 to 2015

    25.____

26. During the five-year period, the annual budget of the Department of Human Resources was GREATER than the annual budget for the Department of Conservation and Environment in _____ of the years.
    A. none   B. one   C. two   D. three

    26.____

27. If the total City X budget increases at the same rate from 2016 to 2017 as it did from 2015 to 2016, the total City X budget for 2017 will be MOST NEARLY _____ million.
    A. $180   B. $200   C. $210   D. $215

    27.____

Questions 28-34.

DIRECTIONS: Questions 28 through 34 are to be answered SOLELY on the basis of the information contained in the graph below which relates to the work of a public agency.

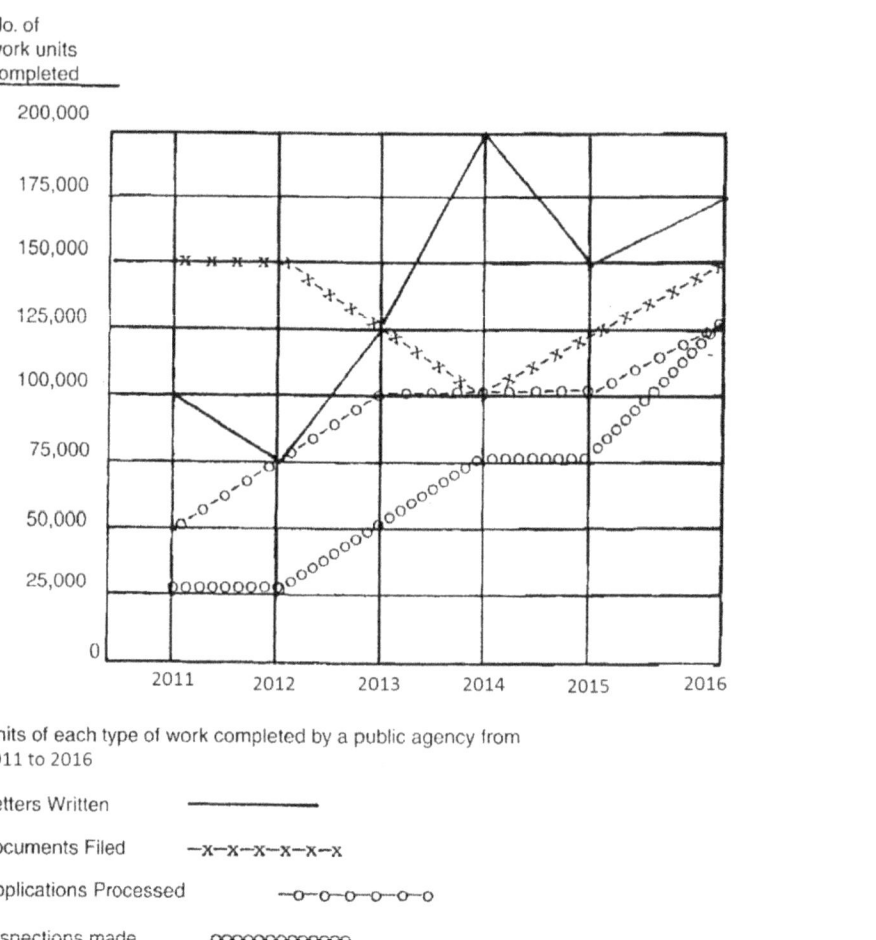

Units of each type of work completed by a public agency from 2011 to 2016

Letters Written ————————
Documents Filed —x—x—x—x—x—x
Applications Processed —o—o—o—o—o—o
Inspections made ooooooooooooo

28. The year for which the number of units of one type of work completed was LESS than it was for the previous year while the number of each of the other types of work completed was MORE than it was for the previous year was
 A. 2012   B. 2013   C. 2014   D. 2015

28.____

29. The number of letters written EXCEEDED the number of applications processed by the same amount in _____ of the years.
 A. two   B. three   C. four   D. five

29.____

30. The year in which the number of each type of work completed was GREATER than in the preceding year was
 A. 2013   B. 2014   C. 2015   D. 2016

30.____

31. The number of applications processed and the number of documents filed wee the SAME in
 A. 2012   B. 2013   C. 2014   D. 2015

31.____

32. The TOTAL number of units of work completed by the agency 32._____
    A. increased in each year after 2011
    B. decreased from the prior year in two of the years after 2011
    C. was the same in two successive years from 2011 to 2016
    D. was less in 2011 than in any of the following years

33. For the year in which the number of letters written was twice as high as it 33._____
    was in 2011, the number of documents filed was _____ it was in 2011.
    A. the same as   B. two-thirds of what
    C. five-sixths of what   D. 1½ times what

34. The variable which was the MOST stable during the period 2011 through 34._____
    2016 was
    A. Inspections Made   B. Letters Written
    C. Documents Filed   D. Applications Processed

Questions 35-41.

DIRECTIONS: Questions 35 through 41 are to be answered SOLELY on the basis of the information in the following passage.

Job evaluation and job rating systems are intended to introduce scientific procedures. Any type of approach, when properly used, will give satisfactory results. The Point System, when properly validated by actual use, is more likely to be suitable for general use than the ranking system. In many aspects, the Factor Comparison Plan is a point system tied to money values. Of course, there may be another system that combines the ranking system with the point system, especially during the initial stages of the development of the program. After the program has been in use for some time, the tendency is to drop off the ranking phrase and continue the use of the point system.

In the ranking system of rating of jobs, every job within the plant is arranged in some order, either from the one with the simplest qualifications to the one with maximum requirements, or in the reverse order. This system should be preceded by careful job analysis and the writing of accurate job descriptions before the rating process is undertaken. It is possible, of course, to take the jobs as they are found in the business enterprise and use the names as they are without any attempt at standardization, and merely rank them according to the general overall impression of the raters. Such a procedure is certain to fall short of what may reasonably be expected of job rating. Another procedure that is in reality merely a modification of the simple rating described above is to establish a series of grades or zones and arrange all the jobs in the plant into groups within these grades and zones. The practice in most common use is to arrange all the jobs in the plant according to their requirements by rating them and then to establish the classifications or groups.

The actual ranking of jobs may be done by one individual, several individuals, or a committee. If several individuals are working independently on the task, it will usually be found that, in general, they agree but that their rankings vary in certain details. A conference between the individuals, with each person giving his reasons why he rated one way or another, usually produces agreement. The detailed job descriptions are particularly helpful when there is disagreement among raters as to the rating of certain jobs. It is not only possible but desirable to have workers participate in the construction of the job description and in rating the job.

35. The MAIN theme of this passage is
    A. the elimination of bias in job rating
    B. the rating of jobs by the ranking system
    C. the need for accuracy in allocating points in the point system
    D. pitfalls to avoid in selecting key jobs in the Factor Comparison Plan

36. The ranking system of rating jobs consists MAINLY of
    A. attaching a point value to each ratable factor of each job prior to establishing an equitable pay scale
    B. arranging every job in the organization in descending order and then following this up with a job analysis of the key jobs
    C. preparing accurate job descriptions after a job analysis and then arranging all jobs either in ascending or descending order based on job requirements
    D. arbitrarily establishing a hierarchy of job classes and grades and then fitting each job into a specific class and grade based on the opinions of unit supervisors

37. The above passage states that the system of classifying jobs MOST used in an organization is to
    A. organize all jobs in the organization in accordance with their requirements and then create categories or clusters of jobs
    B. classify all jobs in the organization according to the titles and ranks by which they are currently known in the organization
    C. establish a pre-arranged series of grades or zones and then fit all jobs into one of the grades or zones
    D. determine the salary currently being paid for each job, and then rank the jobs in order according to salary

38. According to the above passage, experience has shown that when a group of raters is assigned to the job evaluation task and each individual rates independently of the others, the raters GENERALLY
    A. *agree* with respect to all aspects of their rankings
    B. *disagree* with respect to all or nearly all aspects of the rankings
    C. *disagree* on overall ratings but agree on specific rating factors
    D. *agree* on overall rankings but have some variance in some details

39. The above passage states that the use of a detailed job description is of SPECIAL value when
    A. employees of an organization have participated in the preliminary steps involved in actual preparation of the job description
    B. labor representatives are not participating in ranking of the jobs
    C. an individual rater who is unsure of himself is ranking the jobs
    D. a group of raters is having difficulty reaching unanimity with respect to ranking a certain job

40. A comparison of the various rating systems as described in the above passage shows that
    A. the ranking system is not as appropriate for general use as a properly validated point system
    B. the point system is the same as the Factor Comparison Plan except that it places greater emphasis on money
    C. no system is capable of combining the point system and the Factor Comparison Plan
    D. the point system will be discontinued last when used in combination with the Factor Comparison System

41. The above passage implies that the PRINCIPAL reason for creating job evaluation and rating systems was to help
    A. overcome union opposition to existing salary plans
    B. base wage determination on a more objective and orderly foundation
    C. eliminate personal bias on the part of the trained scientific job evaluators
    D. management determine if it was overpricing the various jobs in the organizational hierarchy

42. As a general rule, in a large office it is desirable to have more than one one employee who is able to operate any one machine and more than one office machine capable of performing any one type of required operation. According to this statement, there USUALLY should be
    A. fewer office machines in an office than are necessary for efficient job performance
    B. more office machines in an office than there are employees able to operate them
    C. more types of required operations to be performed than there are machines necessary to their performance
    D. fewer types of required operations to be performed than there are machines capable of performing them

43. The plan of an organization's structure and procedures may appear to be perfectly sound, but the organization may still operate wastefully and with a great amount of friction because of the failure of the people in the organization to work together.
    The MOST valid implication of this statement is that
    A. inefficiency within an organization may be caused by people being directed to do the wrong things
    B. an organization which operates inefficiently might be improved by revising its systems and methods of operations
    C. use of the best methods an organization can devise may not prevent an organization from being inefficient
    D. the people in an organization may not have an appreciation of the high quality of the organization's plan of operations

44. If an employee is to be held responsible for obtaining results, he should be given every reasonable freedom to exercise his own intelligence and initiative to achieve the results expected.
The MOST valid implication of this statement is that
    A. the authority delegated should match the responsibility assigned
    B. achieving results depends upon the individual's willingness to work
    C. the most important aspect of getting a job done is to know how to do it
    D. understanding the requirements of a task is essential to its accomplishment

45. Essentially, an organization is defined as any group of individuals who are cooperating under the direction of executive leadership in an attempt to accomplish certain common objectives.
The one of the following which this statement does NOT include as an essential characteristic of an organization is _____ the members of the group.
    A. cooperation among
    B. proficiency of
    C. authoritative guidance of
    D. goals common to

46. A supervisor, in organizing the work activities of the staff of an office, should recognize that one of the conditions which is expected to promote a high level of interest on the part of an office worker in his job is to assign him to perform a variety of work.
The MOST valid implication of this statement is that
    A. each worker should be taught to perform each type of work in the office
    B. workers should be assigned to perform types of work in which they have expressed interest
    C. a worker who is assigned to perform a single type of work is likely to become bored
    D. some workers are likely to perform several types of work better than other workers are able to

47. Of the following basic guides to effective letter writing, which one would NOT be recommended as a way of improving the quality of business letters?
    A. Use emphatic phrases like *close proximity* and *first and foremost* to round out sentences.
    B. Break up complicated sentences by making short sentences out of dependent clauses.
    C. Replace old-fashioned phrases like *enclosed please find* and *recent date* with a more direct approach.
    D. Personalize letters by using your reader's name at least once in the body of the message.

48. Suppose that you must write a reply letter to a citizen's request for a certain pamphlet printed by your agency. The pamphlet is temporarily unavailable but a new supply will be arriving by December 8 or 9.
Of the following four sentences, which one expresses the MOST positive business letter writing approach?
   A. We cannot send the materials you requested until after December 8.
   B. May we assure you that the materials you requested will be sent as quickly as possible.
   C. We will be sending the materials you requested as soon as our supply is replenished.
   D. We will mail the materials you requested on or shortly after December 8.

48.____

49. Using form letters in business correspondence is LEAST effective when
   A. answering letters on a frequently recurring subject
   B. giving the same information to many addresses
   C. the recipient is only interested in the routine information contained in the form letter
   D. a replay must be keyed to the individual requirements of the intended reader

49.____

50. The ability to write memos and letters is very important in clerical and administrative work. Methodical planning of a reply letter usually involves the following basic steps which are arranged in random order:
I. Determine the purpose of the letter you are about to write.
II. Make an outline of what information your reply letter should contain.
III. Read carefully the letter to be answered to find out its main points.
IV. Assemble the facts to be included in your reply letter.
V. Visualize your intended reader and adapt your letter writing style to him.
If the above-numbered steps were arranged in their proper logical order, the one which would be THIRD in the sequence is
   A. II B. III C. IV D. V

50.____

KEY (CORRECT ANSWERS)

1.	A	11.	C	21.	C	31.	C	41.	B
2.	B	12.	C	22.	D	32.	C	42.	D
3.	C	13.	A	23.	A	33.	B	43.	C
4.	C	14.	B	24.	A	34.	D	44.	A
5.	B	15.	C	25.	B	35.	B	45.	B
6.	C	16.	D	26.	B	36.	C	46.	C
7.	D	17.	B	27.	D	37.	A	47.	A
8.	D	18.	A	28.	B	38.	D	48.	D
9.	B	19.	B	29.	B	39.	D	49.	D
10.	A	20.	D	30.	D	40.	A	50.	A

EXAMINATION SECTION

TEST 1

DIRECTIONS: Each question or incomplete statement is followed by several suggested answers or completions. Select the one that BEST answers the question or completes the statement. *PRINT THE LETTER OF THE CORRECT ANSWER IN THE SPACE AT THE RIGHT.*

Questions 1-4.

DIRECTIONS: Questions 1 through 4 are to be answered SOLELY on the basis of the following passage.

Job analysis combined with performance appraisal is an excellent method of determining training needs of individuals. The steps in this method are to determine the specific duties of the job, to evaluate the adequacy with which the employee performs each of these duties, and finally to determine what significant improvements can be made by training.

The list of duties can be obtained in a number of ways: asking the employee, asking the supervisor, observing the employee, etc. Adequacy of performance can be estimated by the employee, but the supervisor's evaluation must also be obtained. This evaluation will usually be based on observation.

What does the supervisor observe? The employee, while he is working; the employee's work relationships; the ease, speed, and sureness of the employee's actions; the way he applies himself to the job; the accuracy and amount of completed work; its conformity with established procedures and standards; the appearance of the work; the soundness of judgment it shows; and, finally, signs of good or poor communication, understanding, and cooperation among employees.

Such observation is a normal and inseparable part of the everyday job of supervision. Systematically, recorded, evaluated, and summarized, it highlights both general and individual training needs.

1. According to the passage, job analysis may be used by the supervisor in
    A. increasing his own understanding of tasks performed in his unit
    B. increasing efficiency of communication within the organization
    C. assisting personnel experts in the classification of positions
    D. determining in which areas an employee needs more instruction

1.____

2. According to the passage, the FIRST step in determining the training needs of employees is to
    A. locate the significant improvements that can be made by training
    B. determine the specific duties required in a job
    C. evaluate the employee's performance
    D. motivate the employee to want to improve himself

2.____

3. On the basis of the above passage, which of the following is the BEST way for a supervisor to determine the adequacy of employee performance?
   A. Check the accuracy and amount of completed work
   B. Ask the training officer
   C. Observe all aspects of the employee's work
   D. Obtain the employee's own estimate

4. Which of the following is NOT mentioned by the passage as a factor to be taken into consideration in judging the adequacy of employee performance?
   A. Accuracy of completed work
   B. Appearance of completed work
   C. Cooperation among employees
   D. Attitude of the employee toward his supervisor

5. In indexing names of business firms and other organizations, ONE of the rules to be followed is:
   A. The word *and* is considered an indexing unit.
   B. When a firm name includes the full name of a person who is not well-known, the person's first name is considered as the first indexing unit.
   C. Usually the units in a firm name are indexed in the order in which they are written.
   D. When a firm's name is made up of single letters (such as ABC Corp.), the letters taken together are considered more than one indexing unit.

6. Assume that people often come to your office with complaints of errors in your agency's handling of their clients. The employees in your office have the job of listening to these complaints and investigating them. One day, when it is almost closing time, a person comes into your office, apparently very angry, and demands that you take care of his complaint at once.
   Your IMMEDIATE reaction should be to
   A. suggest that he return the following day
   B. find out his name and the nature of his complaint
   C. tell him to write a letter
   D. call over your supervisor

7. Assume that part of your job is to notify people concerning whether their applications for a certain program have been approved or disapproved. However, you do not actually make the decision on approval or disapproval. One day, you answer a telephone call from a woman who states that she has not yet received any word on her application. She goes on to tell you her qualifications for the program. From what she has said, you know that persons with such qualifications are usually approved.
   Of the following, which one is the BEST thing for you to say to her?
   A. "You probably will be accepted, but wait until you receive a letter before trying to join the program."
   B. "Since you seem well qualified, I am sure that your application will be approved."

C. "If you can write us a letter emphasizing your qualifications, it may speed up the process."
D. "You will be notified of the results of your application as soon as a decision has been made."

8. Suppose that one of your duties includes answering specific telephone inquiries. Your superior refers a call to you from an irate person who claims that your agency is inefficient and is wasting taxpayers' money.
   Of the following, the BEST way to handle such a call is to
   A. listen briefly and then hang up without answering
   B. note the caller's comments and tell him that you will transmit them to your superiors
   C. connect the caller with the head of your agency
   D. discuss your own opinions with the caller

8.____

9. An employee has been assigned to open her division head's mail and place it on his desk. One day, the employee opens a letter which she then notices is marked *Personal*.
   Of the following, the BEST action for her to take is to
   A. write *Personal* on the letter and staple the envelope to the back of the letter
   B. ignore the matter and treat the letter the same way as the others
   C. give it to another division head to hold until her own division head comes into the office
   D. leave the letter in the envelope and write *Sorry opened by mistake* on the envelope and initial it

9.____

Questions 10-14.

DIRECTIONS: Questions 10 through 14 each consist of a quotation which contains one word that is incorrectly used because it is not in keeping with the meaning that the quotation is evidently intended to convey. Of the words underlined in each quotation, determine which word is incorrectly used. Then select from among the words lettered A, B, C, and D the word which, when substituted for the incorrectly used word, would BEST help to convey the meaning of the quotation. (Do not indicate a change for an underlined word unless the underlined word is incorrectly used.)

10. Unless reasonable managerial supervision is <u>exercised</u> over office supplies, it is certain that there will be extravagance, <u>rejected</u> items out of stock, <u>excessive</u> prices paid for certain items, and <u>obsolete</u> material in the stockroom.
    A. overlooked   B. immoderate   C. needed   D. instituted

10.____

11. Since <u>office</u> supplies are in such <u>common</u> use, an attitude of indifference about their handling is not <u>unusual</u>. Their importance is often recognized only when they are <u>utilized</u> or out of stock, for office employees must have proper supplies if maximum productivity is to be <u>attained</u>.
    A. plentiful   B. unavailable   C. reduced   D. expected

11.____

12. Anyone <u>effected</u> by paperwork, <u>interested</u> in or engaged in office work, or desiring to improve <u>informational</u> activities can find materials <u>keyed</u> to his needs.
    A. attentive   B. available   C. affected   D. ambitious

13. Information is <u>homogeneous</u> and must therefore be properly classified so that each type may be <u>employed</u> in ways <u>appropriate</u> to its <u>own peculiar</u> properties.
    A. apparent
    B. heterogeneous
    C. consistent
    D. idiosyncratic

14. <u>Intellectual</u> training may seem a <u>formidable</u> phrase, but it means nothing more than the <u>deliberate</u> cultivation of the ability to think, and there is no <u>dark</u> contrast between the intellectual and the practical.
    A. subjective   B. objective   C. sharp   D. vocational

15. The MOST important reason for having a filing system is to
    A. get papers out of the way
    B. have a record of everything that has happened
    C. retain information to justify your actions
    D. enable rapid retrieval of information

16. The system of filing which is used MOST frequently is called _____ filing.
    A. alphabetic
    B. alphanumeric
    C. geographic
    D. numeric

17. One of the clerks under your supervision has been telephoning frequently to tell you that he was taking the day off. Unless there is a real need for it, taking leave which is not scheduled is frowned upon because it upsets the work schedule.
    Under these circumstances, which of the following reasons for taking the day off is MOST acceptable?
    A. "I can't work when my arthritis bothers me."
    B. "I've been pressured with work from my night job and needed the extra time to catch up."
    C. "My family just moved to a new house, and I needed the time to start the repairs."
    D. "Work here has not been challenging, and I've been looking for another job."

18. One of the employees under your supervision, previously a very satisfactory worker, has begun arriving late one or two mornings each week. No explanation has been offered for this change. You call her to your office for a conference. As you are explaining the purpose of the conference and your need to understand this sudden lateness problem, she becomes very angry and states that you have no right to question her.
    Of the following, the BEST course of action for you to take at this point is to

A. inform her in your most authoritarian tone that you are the supervisor and that you have every right to question her
B. end the conference and advise the employee that you will have no further discussion with her until she controls her temper
C. remain calm, try to calm her down, and when she has quieted, explain the reasons for your questions and the need for answers
D. hold your temper; when she has calmed down, tell her that you will not have a tardy worker in your unit and will have her transferred at once

19. Assume that, in the branch of the agency for which you work, you are the only clerical person on the staff with a supervisory title and, in addition, that you are the office manager. On a particular day when all members of the professional staff are away from the building attending an important meeting, an urgent call comes through requesting some confidential information ordinarily released only by professional staff.
Of the following, the MOST reasonable action for you to take is to
    A. decline to give the information because you are not a member of the professional staff
    B. offer to call back after you get permission from the agency director at the main office
    C. advise the caller that you will supply the information as soon as your chief returns
    D. supply the information requested and inform your chief when she returns

20. As a supervisor, you are scheduled to attend an important conference with your superior. However, that day you learn that your very capable assistant is ill and unable to come to work. Several highly sensitive tasks are scheduled for completion on this day.
Of the following, the BEST way to handle this situation is to
    A. tell your supervisor you cannot attend the meeting and ask that it be postponed
    B. assign one of your staff to see that the jobs are completed and turned in
    C. advise your supervisor of the situation and ask what you should do
    D. call the departments for which the work is being done and ask for an extension of time

21. When a decision needs to be made which is likely to affect units other than his own, a supervisor should USUALLY
    A. make such a decision quickly and then discuss it with his supervisor
    B. make such a decision only after careful consultation with his subordinates
    C. discuss the problem with his immediate superior before making such a decision
    D. have his subordinates arrive at such a decision in conference with the subordinates in the other units

22. Assume that, as a supervisor in Division X, you are training Ms. Y, a new employee, to answer the telephone properly.
You should explain that the BEST way to answer is to pick up the receiver and say:

A. "What is your name, please?" B. "May I help you?"
C. "Ms. Y speaking." D. "Division X, Ms. Y speaking."

Questions 23-25.

DIRECTIONS: Questions 23 through 25 consist of sentences in which two words are missing. Examine each sentence, and then choose from below it the words which should be inserted in the blank spaces in order to create a coherent and well-written sentence.

23. Human behavior is far _____ variable, and therefore _____ predictable, than that of any other species. 23.____
    A. less; as   B. less; not   C. more; not   D. more; less

24. The _____ limitation of this method is that the results are based _____ a narrow sample. 24.____
    A. chief; with   B. chief; on   C. only; for   D. only; to

25. Although there _____ a standard procedure for handling these problems, each case often has _____ own unique features. 25.____
    A. are; its   B. are; their   C. is; its   D. is; their

KEY (CORRECT ANSWERS)

1.	D	11.	B
2.	B	12.	C
3.	C	13.	B
4.	D	14.	C
5.	C	15.	D
6.	B	16.	A
7.	D	17.	A
8.	B	18.	C
9.	D	19.	B
10.	C	20.	C

21. C
22. D
23. D
24. B
25. C

TEST 2

DIRECTIONS: Each question or incomplete statement is followed by several suggested answers or completions. Select the one that BEST answers the question or completes the statement. *PRINT THE LETTER OF THE CORRECT ANSWER IN THE SPACE AT THE RIGHT.*

Questions 1-3.

DIRECTIONS: Questions 1 through 3 each consist of a group of four sentences. Read each sentence carefully, and select the one of the four in each group which represents the BEST English usage for business letters and reports.

1. A. The chairman himself, rather than his aides, has reviewed the report. 1.____
   B. The chairman himself, rather than his aides, have reviewed the report.
   C. The chairmen, not the aide, has reviewed the report.
   D. The aide, not the chairmen, have reviewed the report.

2. A. Various proposals were submitted but the decision is not been made. 2.____
   B. Various proposals has been submitted but the decision has not been made.
   C. Various proposals were submitted but the decision is not been made.
   D. Various proposals have been submitted but the decision has not been made.

3. A. Everyone were rewarded for his successful attempt. 3.____
   B. They were successful in their attempts and each of them was rewarded.
   C. Each of them are rewarded for their successful attempts.
   D. The reward for their successful attempts were made to each of them.

4. Which of the following is MOST suited to arrangement in chronological order? 4.____
   A. Applications for various types and levels of jobs
   B. Issues of a weekly publication
   C. Weekly time cards for all employees for the week of April 21
   D. Personnel records for all employees

5. Words that are *synonymous* with a given word ALWAYS _____ the given word. 5.____
   A. have the same meaning as   B. have the same pronunciation as
   C. have the opposite meaning of D. can be rhymed with

Questions 6-11.

DIRECTIONS: Questions 6 through 11 are to be answered on the basis of the following chart showing numbers of errors made by four clerks in one work unit for a half-year period.

55

	Allan	Barry	Cary	David
July	5	4	1	7
August	8	3	9	8
September	7	8	7	5
October	3	6	5	3
November	2	4	4	6
December	5	2	8	4

6. The clerk with the HIGHEST number of errors for the six-month period was
 A. Allan   B. Barry   C. Cary   D. David

7. If the number of errors made by Allan in the six months shown represented one-eighth of the total errors made by the unit during the entire year, what was the TOTAL number of errors made by the unit for the year?
 A. 124   B. 180   C. 240   D. 360

8. The number of errors made by David in November was what FRACTION of the total errors made in November?
 A. 1/3   B. 1/6   C. 3/8   D. 3/16

9. The average number of errors made per month per clerk was MOST NEARLY
 A. 4   B. 5   C. 6   D. 7

10. Of the total number of errors made during the six-month period, the percentage made in August was MOST NEARLY
 A. 2%   B. 4%   C. 23%   D. 4%

11. If the number of errors in the unit were to decrease in the next six months by 30%, what would be MOST NEARLY the total number of errors for the unit for the next six months?
 A. 87   B. 94   C. 120   D. 137

12. The arithmetic mean salary for five employees earning $18,500, $18,300, $18,600, $18,400, and $18,500, respectively is
 A. $18,450   B. $18,460   C. $18,475   D. $18,500

13. Last year, a city department which is responsible for purchasing supplies ordered bond paper in equal quantities from 22 different companies. The price was exactly the same for each company, and the total cost for the 22 orders was $693,113.
 Assuming prices did not change during the year, the cost of EACH order was MOST NEARLY
 A. $31,490   B. $31,495   C. $31,500   D. $31,505

14. A city agency engaged in repair work uses a small part which the city purchases for $0.14 each. Assume that, in a certain year, the total expenditure of the city for this part was $700.
    How MANY of these parts were purchased that year?
    A. 50   B. 200   C. 2,000   D. 5,000

15. The work unit which you supervise is responsible for processing fifteen reports per month.
    If your unit has four clerks and the best worker completes 40% of the reports himself, how many reports would each of the other clerks have to complete if they all do an equal number?
    A. 1   B. 2   C. 3   D. 4

16. Assume that the work unit in which you work has 24 clerks and 18 stenographers. In order to change the ratio of stenographers to clerks so that there is one stenographer for every four clerks, it would be necessary to REDUCE the number of stenographers by
    A. 3   B. 6   C. 9   D. 12

17. Assume that your office is responsible for opening and distributing all the mail of the division. After opening a letter, one of your subordinates notices that it states that there should be an enclosure in the envelope. However, there is no enclosure in the envelope.
    Of the following, the BEST instruction that you can give the clerk is to
    A. call the sender to obtain the enclosure
    B. call the addressee to inform him that the enclosure is missing
    C. note the omission in the margin of the letter
    D. forward the letter without taking any action

18. While opening the envelope containing official correspondence, you accidentally cut the enclosed letter.
    Of the following, the BEST action for you to take is to
    A. leave the material as it is
    B. put it together by using transparent mending tape
    C. keep it together by putting it back in the envelope
    D. keep it together by using paper clips

19. Suppose your supervisor is on the telephone in his office and an applicant arrives for a scheduled interview with him.
    Of the following, the BEST procedure to follow ordinarily is to
    A. informally chat with the applicant in your office until your supervisor has finished his phone conversation
    B. escort him directly into your supervisor's office and have him wait for him there
    C. inform your supervisor of the applicant's arrival and try to make the applicant feel comfortable while waiting
    D. have him hang up his coat and tell him to go directly in to see your supervisor

20. The length of time that files should be kept is GENERALLY
    A. considered to be seven years
    B. dependent upon how much new material has accumulated in the files
    C. directly proportionate to the number of years the office has been in operation
    D. dependent upon the type and nature of the material in the files

21. Cross-referencing a document when you file it means
    A. making a copy of the document and putting the copy into a related file
    B. indicating on the front of the document the name of the person who wrote it, the date it was written, and for what purpose
    C. putting a special sheet or card in a related file to indicate where the document is filed
    D. indicating on the document where it is to be filed

22. Unnecessary handling and recording of incoming mail could be eliminated by
    A. having the person who opens it initial it
    B. indicating on the piece of mail the names of all the individuals who should see it
    C. sending all incoming mail to more than one central location
    D. making a photocopy of each piece of incoming mail

23. Of the following, the office tasks which lend themselves MOST readily to planning and study are
    A. repetitive, occur in volume, and extend over a period of time
    B. cyclical in nature, have small volume, and extend over a short period of time
    C. tasks which occur only once in a great while not according to any schedule, and have large volume
    D. special tasks which occur only once, regardless of their volume and length of time

24. A good recordkeeping system includes all of the following procedures EXCEPT the
    A. filing of useless records
    B. destruction of certain files
    C. transferring of records from one type of file to another
    D. creation of inactive files

25. Assume that, as a supervisor, you are responsible for orienting and training new employees in your unit.
    Which of the following can MOST properly be omitted from your discussions with a new employee?
    A. The purpose of commonly used office forms
    B. Time and leave regulations
    C. Procedures for required handling of routine business calls
    D. The reason the last employee was fired

KEY (CORRECT ANSWERS)

1.	A		11.	A
2.	D		12.	B
3.	B		13.	D
4.	B		14.	D
5.	A		15.	C
6.	C		16.	D
7.	C		17.	C
8.	C		18.	B
9.	B		19.	C
10.	C		20.	D

21. C
22. B
23. A
24. A
25. D

EXAMINATION SECTION

TEST 1

DIRECTIONS: Each question or incomplete statement is followed by several suggested answers or completions. Select the one that BEST answers the question or completes the statement. *PRINT THE LETTER OF THE CORRECT ANSWER IN THE SPACE AT THE RIGHT.*

1. A multi-line telephone with buttons for eight separate lines, plus a *hold* button, is often used when an office requires more than one outside line.
   If you are talking on one line of this type of office phone when another call comes in, what is the procedure to follow if you want to answer the second call but keep the first call on the line?
   Push the
   A. *hold* button at the same time as you push the *pickup* button of the ringing line
   B. *hold* button and then push the *pickup* button of the ringing line
   C. *pickup* button of the ringing line and then push the *hold* button
   D. *pickup* button of the ringing line and push the *hold* button when you return to the original line

   1.____

2. Suppose that you are asked to prepare a petty cash statement for March. The original and one copy are to go to the personnel office. One copy is to go to the fiscal office, and another copy is to go to your supervisor. The last copy is for your files.
   In preparing the statement and the copies, how many sheets of copy paper should you use?
   A. 3   B. 4   C. 5   D. 8

   2.____

3. Which one of the following is the LEAST important advantage of putting the subject of a letter in the heading to the right of the address? It
   A. makes filing of the copy easier
   B. makes more space available in the body of the letter
   C. simplifies distribution of letters
   D. simplifies determination of the subject of the letter

   3.____

4. Of the following, the MOST efficient way to put 100 copies of a one-page letter into 9½" x 4⅛" envelopes for mailing is to fold _____ into an envelope.
   A. each letter and insert it immediately after folding
   B. each letter separately until all 100 are folded; then insert each one
   C. the 100 letters two at a time, then separate them and insert each one
   D. two letters together, slip them apart, and insert each one

   4.____

5. When preparing papers for filing, it is NOT desirable to
   A. smooth papers that are wrinkled
   B. use paper clips to keep related papers together in the files
   C. arrange the papers in the order in which they will be filed
   D. mend torn papers with cellophane tape

6. Of the following, the BEST reason for a clerical unit to have its own duplicating machine is that the unit
   A. uses many forms which it must reproduce internally
   B. must make two copies of each piece of incoming mail for a special file
   C. must make seven copies of each piece of outgoing mail
   D. must type 200 envelopes each month for distribution to the same offices

7. Several offices use the same photocopying machine.
   If each office must pay its share of the cost of running this machine, the BEST way of determining how much of this cost should be charged to each of these offices is to
   A. determine the monthly number of photocopies made by each office
   B. determine the monthly number of originals submitted for photocopying by each office
   C. determine the number of times per day each office uses the photocopying machine
   D. divide the total cost of running the photocopy machine by the total number of offices using the machine

8. Which one of the following would it be BEST to use to indicate that a file folder has been removed from the files for temporary use in another office?
   A(n)
   A. cross-reference card   B. tickler file marker
   C. aperture card   D. out guide

9. Which one of the following is the MOST important objective of filing?
   A. Giving a secretary something to do in her spare time
   B. Making it possible to locate information quickly
   C. Providing a place to store unneeded documents
   D. Keeping extra papers from accumulating on workers' desks

10. If a check has been made out for an incorrect amount, the BEST action for the writer of the check to take is to
    A. erase the original amount and enter the correct amount
    B. cross out the original amount with a single line and enter the correct amount above it
    C. black out the original amount so that it cannot be read and enter the correct amount above it
    D. write a new check

11. Which one of the following BEST describes the usual arrangement of a tickler file?
    A. Alphabetical B. Chronological
    C. Numerical   D. Geographical

11.____

12. Which one of the following is the LEAST desirable filing practice?
    A. Using staples to keep papers together
    B. Filing all material without regard to date
    C. Keeping a record of all materials removed from the files
    D. Writing filing instructions on each paper prior to filing

12.____

13. Assume that one of your duties is to keep records of the office supplies used by your unit for the purpose of ordering new supplies when the old supplies run out.
    The information that will be of MOST help in letting you know when to reorder supplies is the
    A. quantity issued   B. quantity received
    C. quantity on hand   D. stock number

13.____

Questions 14-19.

DIRECTIONS: Questions 14 through 19 consist of sets of names and addresses. In each question, the name and address in Column II should be an exact copy of the name and address in Column I. If there is
a mistake *only* in the name, mark your answer A;
a mistake *only* in the address, mark your answer B;
a mistake in *both* name and address, mark your answer C;
no mistake in either name or address, mark your answer D.

SAMPLE QUESTION

Column I
Michael Filbert
456 Reade Street
New York, N.Y. 10013

Column II
Michael Filbert
645 Reade Street
New York, N.Y. 10013

Since there is a mistake only in the address (the street number should be 456 instead of 645), the answer to the sample question is B.

COLUMN I

COLUMN II

14. Esta Wong
    141 West 68 St.
    New York, N.Y. 10023

    Esta Wang
    141 West 68 St.
    New York,, N.Y. 10023

14.____

15. Dr. Alberto Grosso
    3475 12th Avenue
    Brooklyn, N.Y. 11218

    Dr. Alberto Grosso
    3475 12th Avenue
    Brooklyn, N.Y. 11218

15.____

	Column I	Column II	
16.	Mrs. Ruth Bortlas 482 Theresa Ct. Far Rockaway, N.Y. 11691	Ms. Ruth Bortlas 482 Theresa Ct. Far Rockaway, N.Y. 11169	16.____
17.	Mr. and Mrs. Howard Fox 2301 Sedgwick Avenue Bronx, N.Y. 10468	Mr. and Mrs. Howard Fox 231 Sedgwick Ave. Bronx, N.Y. 10458	17.____
18.	Miss Marjorie Black 223 East 23 Street New York, N.Y. 10010	Miss Margorie Black 223 East 23 Street New York, N.Y. 10010	18.____
19.	Michelle Herman 806 Valley Rd. Old Tappan, N.J. 07675	Michelle Hermann 806 Valley Dr. Old Tappan, N.J. 07675	19.____

Questions 20-25.

DIRECTIONS: Questions 20 through 25 are to be answered SOLELY on the basis of the information in the following passage.

Basic to every office is the need for proper lighting. Inadequate lighting is a familiar cause of fatigue and serves to create a somewhat dismal atmosphere in the office. One requirement of proper lighting is that it be of an appropriate intensity. Intensity is measured in foot-candles. According to the Illuminating Engineering Society of New York, for casual seeing tasks such as in reception rooms, inactive file rooms, and other service areas, it is recommended that the amount of light be 30 foot-candles. For ordinary seeing tasks such as reading and work in active file rooms and in mail rooms, the recommended lighting is 100 foot-candles. For very difficult seeing tasks such as accounting, transcribing, and business machine use, the recommended lighting is 150 foot-candles.

Lighting intensity is only one requirement. Shadows and glare are to be avoided. For example, the larger the proportion of a ceiling filled with lighting units, the more glare-free and comfortable the lighting will be. Natural lighting from windows is not too dependable because on dark wintry days, windows yield little usable light, and on sunny afternoons, the glare from windows may be very distracting. Desks should not face the windows. Finally, the main lighting source ought to be overhead and to the left of the user.

20. According to the above passage, insufficient light in the office may cause 20.____
    A. glare   B. shadows   C. tiredness   D. distraction

21. Based on the above passage, which of the following must be considered when 21.____
    planning lighting arrangements?
    The
    A. amount of natural light present
    B. amount of work to be done
    C. level of difficulty of work to be done
    D. type of activity to be carried out

22. It can be inferred from the above passage that a well-coordinated lighting scheme is LIKELY to result in
    A. greater employee productivity
    B. elimination of light reflection
    C. lower lighting cost
    D. more use of natural light

23. Of the following, the BEST title for the above passage is
    A. Characteristics of Light
    B. Light Measurement Devices
    C. Factors to Consider When Planning Lighting Systems
    D. Comfort vs. Cost When Devising Lighting Arrangements

24. According to the above passage, a foot-candle is a measurement of the
    A. number of bulbs used
    B. strength of the light
    C. contrast between glare and shadow
    D. proportion of the ceiling filled with lighting units

25. According to the above passage, the number of foot-candles of light that would be needed to copy figures onto a payroll is _____ foot-candles.
    A. less than 30   B. 30   C. 100   D. 150

KEY (CORRECT ANSWERS)

1.	B	11.	B
2.	B	12.	B
3.	B	13.	C
4.	A	14.	A
5.	B	15.	D
6.	A	16.	C
7.	A	17.	B
8.	D	18.	A
9.	B	19.	C
10.	D	20.	C

21.	D
22.	A
23.	C
24.	B
25.	D

TEST 2

DIRECTIONS: Each question or incomplete statement is followed by several suggested answers or completions. Select the one that BEST answers the question or completes the statement. *PRINT THE LETTER OF THE CORRECT ANSWER IN THE SPACE AT THE RIGHT.*

1. Assume that a supervisor has three subordinates who perform clerical tasks. One of the employees retires and is replaced by someone who is transferred from another unit in the agency. The transferred employee tells the supervisor that she has worked as a clerical employee for two years and understands clerical operations quite well. The supervisor then assigns the transferred employee to a desk, tells the employee to begin working, and returns to his own desk.
   The supervisor's action in this situation is
   A. *proper*; experienced clerical employees do not require training when they are transferred to new assignments
   B. *improper*; before the supervisor returns to his desk, he should tell the other two subordinates to watch the transferred employee perform the work
   C. *proper*; if the transferred employee makes any mistakes, she will bring them to the supervisor's attention
   D. *improper*; the supervisor should find out what clerical tasks the transferred employee has performed and give her instruction in those which are new or different

   1._____

2. Assume that you are falling behind in completing your work assignments and you believe that your workload is too heavy.
   Of the following, the BEST course of action for you to take FIRST is to
   A. discuss the problem with your supervisor
   B. decide which of your assignments can be postponed
   C. try to get some of your co-workers to help you out
   D. plan to take some of the work home with you in order to catch up

   2._____

3. Suppose that one of the clerks under your supervision is filling in monthly personnel forms. She asks you to explain a particular personnel regulation which is related to various items on the forms. You are not thoroughly familiar with the regulation.
   Of the following responses you may make, the one which will gain the MOST respect from the clerk and which is generally the MOST advisable is to
   A. tell the clerk to do the best she can and that you will check her work later
   B. inform the clerk that you are not sure of a correct explanation but suggest a procedure for her to follow
   C. give the clerk a suitable interpretation so that she will think you are familiar with all regulations
   D. tell the clerk that you will have to read the regulation more thoroughly before you can give her an explanation

   3._____

4. Charging out records until a specified due date, with prompt follow-up if they are not returned, is a
   A. *good* idea; it may prevent the records from being kept needlessly on someone's desk for long periods of time
   B. *good* idea; it will indicate the extent of your authority to other departments
   C. *poor* idea; the person borrowing the material may make an error because of the pressure put upon him to return the records
   D. *poor* idea; other departments will feel that you do not trust them with the records and they will be resentful

4.____

Questions 5-9.

DIRECTIONS: Questions 5 through 9 consist of three lines of code letters and numbers. The numbers on each line should correspond with the code letters on the same line in accordance with the table below.

Code Letter	P	L	I	J	B	O	H	U	C	G
Corresponding Letter	0	1	2	3	4	5	6	7	8	9

On some of the lines, an error exists in the coding. Compare the letters and numbers in each question carefully. If you find an error or errors on
only one of the lines in the question, mark your answer A;
any two lines in the question, mark your answer B;
all three lines in the question, mark your answer C;
none of the lines in the question, mark your answer D.

SAMPLE QUESTION
JHOILCP   3652180
BICLGUP   4286970
UCIBHLJ   5824613

In the above sample, the first line is correct since each code letter listed has the correct corresponding number. On the second line, an error exists because code letter L should have the number 1 instead of the number 6. On the third line, an error exists because the code letter U should have the number 7 instead of the number 5. Since there are errors on two of the three lines, the correct answer is B.

5. BULJCIP   4713920
    HIGPOUL   6290571
    OCUHJJBI   5876342

5.____

6. CUBLOIJ   8741023
    LCLGCLB   1818914
    JPUHIOC   3076158

6.____

7. OIJGCBPO   52398405
    UHPBLIOP   76041250
    CLUIPGPC   81720908

7.____

8.	BPCOUOJI	40875732	8.____
	UOHCIPLB	75682014	
	GLHUUCBJ	92677843	

9.	HOIOHJLH	65256361	9.____
	IOJJHHBP	25536640	
	OJHBJOPI	53642502	

Questions 10-13.

DIRECTIONS: Questions 10 through 13 are to be answered SOLELY on the basis of the information given in the following passage.

The mental attitude of the employee toward safety is exceedingly important in preventing accidents. All efforts designed to keep safety on the employee's mind and to keep accident prevention a live subject in the office will help substantially in a safety program. Although it may seem strange, it is common for people to be careless. Therefore, safety education is a continuous process.

Safety rules should be explained, and the reasons for their rigid enforcement should be given to employees. Telling employees to be careful or giving similar general safety warnings and slogans is probably of little value. Employees should be informed of basic safety fundamentals. This can be done through staff meetings, informal suggestions to employees, movies, and safety instruction cards. Safety instruction cards provide the employees with specific suggestions about safety and serve as a series of timely reminder helping to keep safety on the minds of employees. Pictures, posters, and cartoon sketches on bulletin boards that are located in areas continually used by employees arouse the employees' interest in safety. It is usually good to supplement this type of safety promotion with intensive individual follow-up.

10. The above passage implies that the LEAST effective of the following safety measures is
    A. rigid enforcement of safety rules
    B. getting employees to think in terms of safety
    C. elimination of unsafe conditions in the office
    D. telling employees to stay alert at all times

10.____

11. The reason given by the passage for maintaining ongoing safety education is that
    A. people are often careless
    B. office tasks are often dangerous
    C. the value of safety slogans increases with repetition
    D. safety rules change frequently

11.____

12. Which one of the following safety aids is MOST likely to be preferred by the passage? A
    A. cartoon of a man tripping over a carton and yelling, *Keep aisles clear!*
    B. poster with a large number one and a caption saying, *Safety First*

12.____

C. photograph of a very neatly arranged office
D. large sign with the word *THINK* in capital letters

13. Of the following, the BEST title for the above passage is   13.____
    A. Basic Safety Fundamentals
    B. Enforcing Safety Among Careless Employees
    C. Attitudes Toward Safety
    D. Making Employees Aware of Safety

Questions 14-21.

DIRECTIONS: Questions 14 through 21 are to be answered SOLELY on the basis of the information and chart given below.

The following chart shows expenses in five selected categories for a one-year period, expressed as percentages of these same expenses during the previous year. The chart compares two different offices. In Office T (represented by ▓▓▓▓), a cost reduction program has been tested for the past year. The other office, Office Q (represented by ▨▨▨), served as a control, in that no special effort was made to reduce costs during the past year.

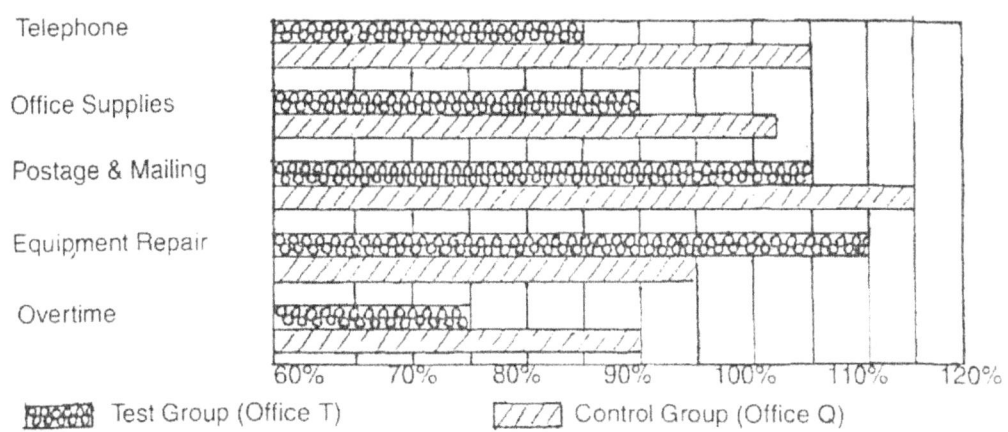

RESULTS OF OFFICE COST REDUCTION PROGRAM
Expenses of Test and Control Groups for 2020
Expressed as Percentages of Same Expenses for 2019

14. In Office T, which category of expense showed the greatest percentage   14.____
    REDUCTION from 2019 to 2020?
    A. Telephone   B. Office Supplies
    C. Postage & Mailing   D. Overtime

15. In which expense category did Office T show the BEST results in percentage   15.____
    terms when compared to Office Q?
    A. Telephone   B. Office Supplies
    C. Postage & Mailing   D. Overtime

16. According to the above chart, the cost reduction program was LEAST effective for the expense category of
    A. Office Supplies
    B. Postage & Mailing
    C. Equipment Repair
    D. Overtime

17. Office T's telephone costs went down during 2020 by approximately how many percentage points?
    A. 15
    B. 20
    C. 85
    D. 104

18. Which of the following changes occurred in expenses for Office Supplies in Office Q in the year 2020 as compared with the year 2019?
    They
    A. increased by more than 100%
    B. remained the same
    C. decreased by a few percentage points
    D. increased by a few percentage points

19. For which of the following expense categories do the results in Office T and the results in Office Q differ MOST NEARLYY by 10 percentage points?
    A. Telephone
    B. Postage & Mailing
    C. Equipment Repair
    D. Overtime

20. In which expense category did Office Q's costs show the GREATEST percentage increase in 2020?
    A. Telephone
    B. Office Supplies
    C. Postage & Mailing
    D. Equipment Repair

21. In Office T, by approximately what percentage did overtime expense change during the past year? It
    A. *increased* by 15%
    B. *increased* by 75%
    C. *decreased* by 10%
    D. *decreased* by 25%

22. In a particular agency, there were 160 accidents in 2017. Of these accidents, 75% were due to unsafe acts and the rest were due to unsafe conditions. In the following year, a special safety program was established. The number of accidents in 2019 due to unsafe acts was reduced to 35% of what it had been in 2017.
    How many accidents due to unsafe acts were there in 2019?
    A. 20
    B. 36
    C. 42
    D. 56

23. At the end of every month, the petty cash fund of Agency A is reimbursed for payments made from the fund during the month. During the month of February, the amounts paid from the fund were entered on receipts as follows: 10 bus fares of $3.50 each and one taxi fare of $35.00. At the end of the month, the money left in the fund was in the following denominations: 15 ten-dollar bills, 10 one-dollar bills, 40 quarters, and 100 dimes.
    If the petty cash fund is reduced by 20% for the following month, how much money will there be available in the petty cash fund for March?
    A. $110.00
    B. $200.00
    C. $215.00
    D. $250.00

24. The one of the following records which it would be MOST advisable to keep in alphabetical order is a
    A. continuous listing of phone messages, including time and caller, for your supervisor
    B. listing of individuals currently employed by your agency in a particular title
    C. record of purchases paid for by the petty cash fund
    D. dated record of employees who have borrowed material from the files in your office

25. Assume that you have been asked to copy by hand a column of numbers with two decimal places from one record to another. Each number consists of three, four, and five digits.
    In order to copy them quickly and accurately, you should copy
    A. each number exactly, making sure that the column of digits farthest to the right is in a straight line and all other columns are lined up
    B. the column of digits farthest to the right and then copy the next column of digits moving from right to left
    C. the column of digits farthest to the left and then copy the next column of digits moving from left to right
    D. the digits to the right of each decimal point and then copy the digits to the left of each decimal point

KEY (CORRECT ANSWERS)

1.	D	11.	A
2.	A	12.	A
3.	D	13.	D
4.	A	14.	D
5.	A	15.	A
6.	C	16.	C
7.	D	17.	A
8.	B	18.	D
9.	C	19.	B
10.	D	20.	C

21.	D
22.	C
23.	B
24.	B
25.	A

EXAMINATION SECTION
TEST 1

DIRECTIONS: Each question or incomplete statement is followed by several suggested answers or completions. Select the one that BEST answers the question or completes the statement. *PRINT THE LETTER OF THE CORRECT ANSWER IN THE SPACE AT THE RIGHT.*

Questions 1-10.

WORD MEANING

DIRECTIONS: Each question from 1 to 10 contains a word in capitals followed by four suggested meanings of the word. For each question, choose the best meaning. *PRINT THE LETTER OF THE CORRECT ANSWER IN THE SPACE AT THE RIGHT.*

1. ACCURATE
    A. correct   B. useful   C. afraid   D. careless

2. ALTER
    A. copy   B. change   C. report   D. agree

3. DOCUMENT
    A. outline   B. agreement   C. blueprint   D. record

4. INDICATE
    A. listen   B. show   C. guess   D. try

5. INVENTORY
    A. custom   B. discovery   C. warning   D. list

6. ISSUE
    A. annoy   B. use up   C. give out   D. gain

7. NOTIFY
    A. inform   B. promise   C. approve   D. strengthen

8. ROUTINE
    A. path   B. mistake   C. habit   D. journey

9. TERMINATE
    A. rest   B. start   C. deny   D. end

10. TRANSMIT
    A. put in   B. send   C. stop   D. go across

Questions 11-15.

READING COMPREHENSION

DIRECTIONS: Questions 11 through 15 test how well you understand what you read. It will be necessary for you to read carefully because your answers to these questions should be based ONLY on the information given in the following paragraphs.

The recipient gains an impression of a typewritten letter before he begins to read the message. Pastors which provide for a good first impression include margins and spacing that are visually pleasing, formal parts of the letter which are correctly placed according to the style of the letter, copy which is free of obvious erasures and over-strikes, and transcript that is even and clear. The problem for the typist is that of how to produce that first, positive impression of her work.

There are several general rules which a typist can follow when she wishes to prepare a properly spaced letter on a sheet of letter-head. Ordinarily, the width of a letter should not be less than four inches nor more than six inches. The side margins should also have a desirable relation to the bottom margin and the space between the letterhead and the body of the letter. Usually the most appealing arrangement is when the side margins are even and the bottom margin is slightly wider than the side margins. In some offices, however, standard line length is used for all business letters, and the secretary then varies the spacing between the date line and the inside address according to the length of the letter.

11. The BEST title for the above paragraphs would be:

    A. Writing Office Letters
    B. Making Good First Impressions
    C. Judging Well-Typed Letters
    D. Good Placing and Spacing for Office Letters

12. According to the above paragraphs, which of the following might be considered the way in which people very quickly judge the quality of work which has been typed? By

    A. measuring the margins to see if they are correct
    B. looking at the spacing and cleanliness of the typescript
    C. scanning the body of the letter for meaning
    D. reading the date line and address for errors

13. What, according to the above paragraphs, would be definitely UNDESIRABLE as the average line length of a typed letter?

    A. 4"   B. 5"   C. 6"   D. 7"

14. According to the above paragraphs, when the line length is kept standard, the secretary

    A. does not have to vary the spacing at all since this also is standard
    B. adjusts the spacing between the date line and inside address for different lengths of letters
    C. uses the longest line as a guideline for spacing between the date line and inside address
    D. varies the number of spaces between the lines

15. According to the above paragraphs, side margins are MOST pleasing when they

    A. are even and somewhat smaller than the bottom margin
    B. are slightly wider than the bottom margin
    C. vary with the length of the letter
    D. are figured independently from the letterhead and the body of the letter

Questions 16-20.

CODING

DIRECTIONS:

Name of Applicant	H A N G S B R U K E	
Test Code	c o m p l e x i t y	
File Number	0 1 2 3 4 5 6 7 8 9	

Assume that each of the above capital letters is the first letter of the name of an Applicant, that the small letter directly beneath each capital letter is the test code for the Applicant, and that the number directly beneath each code letter is the file number for the Applicant.

In each of the following Questions 16 through 20, the test code letters and the file numbers in Columns 2 and 3 should correspond to the capital letters in Column 1. For each question, look at each column carefully and mark your answer as follows:

If there is an error only in Column 2, mark your answer A.
If there is an error only in Column 3, mark your answer B.
If there is an error in both Columns 2 and 3, mark your answer C.
If both Columns 2 and 3 are correct, mark your answer D.

The following sample question is given to help you understand the procedure.

SAMPLE QUESTION

Column 1	Column 2	Column 3
AKEHN	otyci	18902

In Column 2, the final test code letter *i.* should be m. Column 3 is correctly coded to Column 1. Since there is an error only in Column 2, the answer is A.

	Column 1	Column 2	Column 3
16.	NEKKU	mytti	29987
17.	KRAEB	txyle	86095
18.	ENAUK	ymoit	92178
19.	REANA	xeomo	69121
20.	EKHSE	ytcxy	97049

Questions 21-30.

ARITHMETICAL REASONING

21. If a secretary answered 28 phone calls and typed the addresses for 112 credit statements in one morning, what is the ratio of phone calls answered to credit statements typed for that period of time?

    A. 1:4   B. 1:7   C. 2:3   D. 3:5

22. According to a suggested filing system, no more than 10 folders should be filed behind any one file guide and from 15 to 25 file guides should be used in each file drawer for easy finding and filing.
    The maximum number of folders that a five-drawer file cabinet can hold to allow easy finding and filing is

    A. 550   B. 750   C. 1,100   D. 1,250

23. An employee had a starting salary of $25,804. He received a salary increase at the end of each year, and at the end of the seventh year his salary was $33,476.
    What was his average annual increase in salary over these seven years?

    A. $1,020   B. $1,076   C. $1,096   D. $1,144

24. The 55 typists and 28 senior clerks in a certain city agency were paid a total of $1,943,200 in salaries last year.
    If the average annual salary of a typist was $22,400 the average annual salary of a senior clerk was

    A. $25,400   B. $26,600   C. $26,800   D. $27,000

25. A typist has been given a three page report to type. She has finished typing the first two pages. The first page has 283 words, and the second page has 366 words.
    If the total report consists of 954 words, how many words will she have to type on the third page of the report?

    A. 202   B. 287   C. 305   D. 313

26. In one day, Clerk A processed 30% more forms than Clerk 8, and Clerk C processed 1 1/4 times as many forms as Clerk A. If Clerk B processed 40 forms, how many more forms were processed by Clerk C than Clerk B?

    A. 12   B. 13   C. 21   D. 25

27. A clerk who earns a gross salary of $452 every two weeks has the following deductions taken from her paycheck:
    15% for City, State, Federal taxes; 2 1/2% for Social Security; $1.30 for health insurance; and $6.00 for union dues. The amount of her take-home pay is

    A. $256.20   B. $312.40   C. $331.60   D. $365.60

28. In 2020, a city agency spent $2,000 to buy pencils at a cost of $5.00 a dozen.
    If the agency used 3/4 of these pencils in 2020 and used the same number of pencils in 2021, how many more pencils did it have to buy to have enough pencils for all of 2021?

    A. 1,200   B. 2,400   C. 3,600   D. 4,800

29. A clerk who worked in Agency X earned the following salaries: $20,140 the first year, $21,000 the second year, and $21,920 the third year. Another clerk who worked in Agency Y for three years earned $21,100 a year for two years and $21,448 the third year. The difference between the average salaries received by both clerks over a three-year period is

    A. $196   B. $204   C. $348   D. $564

30. An employee who works over 40 hours in any week receives overtime payment for the extra hours at time and one-half (1 1/2 times) his hourly rate of pay. An employee who earns $13.60 an hour works a total of 45 hours during a certain week.
    His total pay for that week would be

    A. $564.40   B. $612.00   C. $646.00   D. $812.00

Questions 31-35.

RELATED INFORMATION

31. To tell a newly-employed clerk to fill a top drawer of a four-drawer cabinet with heavy folders which will be often used and to keep lower drawers only partly filled is

    A. *good,* because a tall person would have to bend unnecessarily if he had to use a lower drawer
    B. *bad,* because the file cabinet may tip over when the top drawer is opened
    C. *good,* because it is the most easily reachable drawer for the average person
    D. *bad,* because a person bending down at another drawer may accidentally bang his head on the bottom of the drawer when he straightens up

32. If a senior typist or senior clerk has requisitioned a *ream* of paper in order to duplicate a single page office announcement, how many announcements can be printed from the one package of paper?

    A. 200   B. 500   C. 700   0. 1,000

33. Your supervisor has asked you to locate a telephone number for an attorney named Jones, whose office is located at 311 Broadway, and whose name is not already listed in your files.
    The BEST method for finding the number would be for you to

    A. call the information operator and have her get it for you
    B. look in the alphabetical directory (white pages) under the name Jones at 311 Broadway
    C. refer to the heading Attorney in the yellow pages for the name Jones at 311 Broadway
    D. ask your supervisor who referred her to Mr. Jones, then call that person for the number

34. An example of material that should NOT be sent by first class mail is a

    A. email copy of a letter   B. post card
    C. business reply card   D. large catalogue

35. In the operations of a government agency, a voucher is ORDINARILY used to
    A. refer someone to the agency for a position or assignment
    B. certify that an agency's records of financial trans-actions are accurate
    C. order payment from agency funds of a stated amount to an individual
    D. enter a statement of official opinion in the records of the agency

Questions 36-40.

ENGLISH USAGE

DIRECTIONS: Each question from 36 through 40 contains a sentence. Read each sentence carefully to decide whether it is correct. Then, in the space at the right, mark your answer:

(A) if the sentence is incorrect because of bad grammar or sentence structure

(B) if the sentence is incorrect because of bad punctuation

(C) if the sentence is incorrect because of bad capitalization

(D) if the sentence is correct

Each incorrect sentence has only one type of error. Consider a sentence correct if it has no errors, although there may be other correct ways of saying the same thing.

SAMPLE QUESTION I: One of our clerks were promoted yesterday.

The subject of this sentence is one, so the verb should be *was promoted* instead of *were promoted*. Since the sentence is incorrect because of bad grammar, the answer to Sample Question I is (A).

SAMPLE QUESTION II: Between you and me, I would prefer not going there.

Since this sentence is correct, the answer to Sample Question II is (D).

36. The National alliance of Businessmen is trying to persuade private businesses to hire youth in the summertime.

37. The supervisor who is on vacation, is in charge of processing vouchers.

38. The activity of the committee at its conferences is always stimulating.

39. After checking the addresses again, the letters went to the mailroom.

40. The director, as well as the employees, are interested in sharing the dividends.

Questions 41-45.

FILING

DIRECTIONS: Each question from 41 through 45 contains four names. For each question, choose the name that should be FIRST if the four names are to be arranged in alphabetical order in accordance with the Rules for Alphabetical Filing given below. Read these rules carefully. Then, for each question, indicate in the space at the right the letter before the name that should be FIRST in alphabetical order.

RULES FOR ALPHABETICAL FILING

Names of People

(1) *The names of people are filed in strict alphabetical order, first according to the last name, then according to first name or initial, and finally according to middle name or initial. FOR EXAMPLE: George Allen comes before Edward Bell, and Leonard P. Reston comes before Lucille B. Reston.*

(2) *When last names are the same, FOR EXAMPLE, A. Green and Agnes Green, the one with the initial comes before the one with the name written out when the first initials are identical.*

(3) *When first and last names are alike and the middle name is given, FOR EXAMPLE, John David Doe and John Devoe Doe, the names should be filed in the alphabetical order of the middle names.*

(4) *When first and last names are the same, a name without a middle initial comes before one with a middle name or initial. FOR EXAMPLE, John Doe comes before both John A. Doe and John Alan Doe.*

(5) *When first and last names are the same, a name with a middle initial comes before one with a middle name beginning with the same initial. FOR EXAMPLE: Jack R. Hertz comes before Jack Richard Hertz.*

(6) *Prefixes such as De, O', Mac, Mc, and Van are filed as written and are treated as part of the names to which they are connected. FOR EXAMPLE: Robert O'Dea is filed before David Olsen.*

(7) *Abbreviated names are treated as if they were spelled out. FOR EXAMPLE: Chas. is filed as Charles and Thos. is filed as Thomas.*

(8) *Titles and designations such as Dr., Mr., and Prof, are disregarded in filing.*

Names of Organizations

(1) *The names of business organizations are filed according to the order in which each word in the name appears. When an organization name bears the name of a person, it is filed according to the rules for filing names of people as given above. FOR EXAMPLE: William Smith Service Co. comes before Television Distributors, Inc.*

(2) Where bureau, board, office, or department appears as the first part of the title of a governmental agency, that agency should be filed under the word in the title expressing the chief function of the agency FOR EXAMPLE: Bureau of the Budget would be filed as if written Budget, (Bureau of the). The Department of Personnel would be filed as if written Personnel, (Department of).

(3) When the following words are part of an organization, they are disregarded: the, of, and.

(4) When there are numbers in a name, they are treated as if they were spelled out. FOR EXAMPLE: 10th Street Bootery is filed as Tenth Street Bootery.

SAMPLE QUESTION:
- A. Jane Earl (2)
- B. James A. Earle (4)
- C. James Earl (1)
- D. J. Earle (3)

The numbers in parentheses show the proper alphabetical order in which these names should be filed. Since the name that should be filed FIRST is James Earl, the answer to the Sample Question is (C).

41.
- A. Majorca Leather Goods
- B. Robert Maiorca and Sons
- C. Maintenance Management Corp.
- D. Majestic Carpet Mills

42.
- A. Municipal Telephone Service
- B. Municipal Reference Library
- C. Municipal Credit Union
- D. Municipal Broadcasting System

43.
- A. Robert B. Pierce
- B. R. Bruce Pierce
- C. Ronald Pierce
- D. Robert Bruce Pierce

44.
- A. Four Seasons Sports Club
- B. 14th. St. Shopping Center
- C. Forty Thieves Restaurant
- D. 42nd St. Theaters

45.
- A. Franco Franceschini
- B. Amos Franchini
- C. Sandra Franceschia
- D. Lilie Franchinesca

Questions 46-50.

SPELLING

DIRECTIONS: In each question, one of the words is misspelled. Select the letter of the misspelled word. *PRINT THE LETTER OF THE CORRECT ANSWER IN THE SPACE AT THE RIGHT.*

46.
- A. option
- B. extradite
- C. comparitive
- D. jealousy

47.
- A. handicaped
- B. assurance
- C. sympathy
- D. speech

48. A. recommend   B. carraige
    C. disapprove   D. independent

49. A. ingenuity   B. tenet (opinion)
    C. uncanny   D. intrigueing

50. A. arduous   B. hideous
    C. iervant   D. companies

KEY (CORRECT ANSWERS)

1. A	11. D	21. A	31. B	41. C
2. B	12. B	22. D	32. B	42. D
3. D	13. D	23. C	33. C	43. B
4. B	14. B	24. A	34. D	44. D
5. D	15. A	25. C	35. C	45. C
6. C	16. B	26. D	36. C	46. C
7. A	17. C	27. D	37. B	47. A
8. C	18. D	28. B	38. D	48. B
9. D	19. A	29. A	39. A	49. D
10. B	20. C	30. C	40. A	50. C

EXAMINATION SECTION
TEST 1

DIRECTIONS: Each question or incomplete statement is followed by several suggested answers or completions. Select the one that BEST answers the question or completes the statement. *PRINT THE LETTER OF THE CORRECT ANSWER IN THE SPACE AT THE RIGHT.*

Questions 1-5.

DIRECTIONS: Questions 1 through 5 consist of a sentence with an underlined word. For each question, select the choice that is CLOSEST in meaning to the underlined word.

EXAMPLE
This division reviews the fiscal reports of the agency.
In this sentence, the word *fiscal* means MOST NEARLY
    A. financial   B. critical   C. basic   D. personnel
The correct answer is A. "financial" because "financial" is closest to *fiscal*. Therefore, the answer is A.

1. Every good office worker needs basic skills.
   The word *basic* in this sentence means
     A. fundamental B. advanced C. unusual D. outstanding

   1.____

2. He turned out to be a good instructor.
   The word *instructor* in this sentence means
     A. student B. worker C. typist D. teacher

   2.____

3. The quantity of work in the office was under study.
   In this sentence, the word *quantity* means
     A. amount B. flow C. supervision D. type

   3.____

4. The morning was spent examining the time records.
   In this sentence, the word *examining* means
     A. distributing B. collecting C. checking D. filing

   4.____

5. The candidate filled in the proper spaces on the form.
   In this sentence, the word *proper* means
     A. blank B. appropriate C. many D. remaining

   5.____

Questions 6-8.

DIRECTIONS: Questions 6 through 8 are to be answered SOLELY on the basis of the information contained in the following paragraph.

The increase in the number of public documents in the last two centuries closely matches the increase in population in the United States. The great number of public documents has become a serious threat to their usefulness. It is necessary to have programs which will reduce the number of public documents that are kept and which will, at the same time, assure keeping those that have value. Such programs need a great deal of thought to have any success.

6. According to the above paragraph, public documents may be less useful if 6.____
   A. the files are open to the public
   B. the record room is too small
   C. the copying machine is operated only during normal working hours
   D. too many records are being kept

7. According to the above paragraph, the growth of the population in the United 7.____
   States has matched the growth in the quantity of public documents for a period
   of MOST NEARLY _____ years.
   A. 50 B. 100 C. 200 D. 300

8. According to the above paragraph, the increased number of public documents 8.____
   has made it necessary to
   A. find out which public documents are worth keeping
   B. reduce the great number of public documents by decreasing government services
   C. eliminate the copying of all original public documents
   D. avoid all new copying devices

Questions 9-10.

DIRECTIONS: Questions 9 and 10 are to be answered SOLELY on the basis of the information contained in the following paragraph.

The work goals of an agency can best be reached if the employees understand and agree with these goals. One way to gain such understanding and agreement is for management to encourage and seriously consider suggestions from employees in the setting of agency goals.

9. On the basis of the above paragraph, the BEST way to achieve the work goals 9.____
   of an agency is to
   A. make certain that employees work as hard as possible
   B. study the organizational structure of the agency
   C. encourage employees to think seriously about the agency's problems
   D. stimulate employee understanding of the work goals

10. On the basis of the above paragraph, understanding and agreement with agency 10._____
 goals can be gained by
  A. allowing the employees to set agency goals
  B. reaching agency goals quickly
  C. legislative review of agency operations
  D. employee participation in setting agency goals

Questions 11-15.

DIRECTIONS: Each of Questions 11 through 15 consists of a group of four words. One word in each group is incorrectly spelled. For each question, print the letter of the correct answer in the space at the right that is the same as the letter next to the word which is INCORRECTLY spelled.

EXAMPLE

A. housing   B. certain   C. budgit   D. money

The word "budgit" is incorrectly spelled, because the correct spelling should be "budget." Therefore, the correct answer is C.

11.	A. sentince	B. bulletin	C. notice	D. definition	11._____
12.	A. appointment	B. exactly	C. typest	D. light	12._____
13.	A. penalty	B. suparvise	C. consider	D. division	13._____
14.	A. schedule	B. accurate	C. corect	D. simple	14._____
15.	A. suggestion	B. installed	C. proper	D. agincy	15._____

Questions 16-20.

DIRECTIONS: Each Question 16 through 20 consists of a sentence which may be
  A. incorrect because of bad word usage, or
  B. incorrect because of bad punctuation, or
  C. incorrect because of bad spelling, or
  D. correct
 Read each sentence carefully. Then print in the space at the right A, B, C, or D, according to the answer you choose from the four choices listed above. There is only one type of error in each incorrect sentence. If there is no error, the sentence is correct.

EXAMPLE

George Washington was the father of his contry.
This sentence is incorrect because of bad spelling ("contry" instead of "country").
Therefore, the answer is C.

16. The assignment was completed in record time but the payroll for it has not yet been preparid.   16._____

17. The operator, on the other hand, is willing to learn me how to use the mimeograph.   17._____

18. She is the prettiest of the three sisters.   18._____

19. She doesn't know; if the mail has arrived.   19._____

20. The doorknob of the office door is broke.   20._____

21. A clerk can process a form in 15 minutes.
    How many forms can that clerk process in six hours?
    A. 10   B. 21   C. 24   D. 90   21._____

22. An office staff consists of 120 people. Sixty of them have been assigned to a special project. Of the remaining staff, 20 answer the mail, 10 handle phone calls, and the rest operate the office machines.
    The number of people operating the office machines is
    A. 20   B. 30   C. 40   D. 45   22._____

23. An office worker received 65 applications but on the first day had to return 26 of them for being incomplete and on the second day 25 had to be returned for being incomplete.
    How many applications did NOT have to be returned?
    A. 10   B. 12   C. 14   D. 16   23._____

24. An office worker answered 63 phone calls in one day and 91 phone calls the next day.
    For these 2 days, what was the average number of phone calls he answered per day?
    A. 77   B. 28   C. 82   D. 93   24._____

25. An office worker processed 12 vouchers of $8.50 each, 3 vouchers of $3.68 each, and 2 vouchers of $1.29 each.
    The TOTAL dollar amount of these vouchers is
    A. $116.04   B. $117.52   C. $118.62   D. $119.04   25._____

KEY (CORRECT ANSWERS)

1. A
2. D
3. A
4. C
5. B

6. D
7. C
8. A
9. D
10. D

11. A
12. C
13. B
14. C
15. D

16. C
17. A
18. D
19. B
20. A

21. C
22. B
23. C
24. A
25. C

TEST 2

DIRECTIONS: Each question or incomplete statement is followed by several suggested answers or completions. Select the one that BEST answers the question or completes the statement. *PRINT THE LETTER OF THE CORRECT ANSWER IN THE SPACE AT THE RIGHT.*

Questions 1-5.

DIRECTIONS: Each Question from 1 through 5 lists four names. The names may not be exactly the same. Compare the names in each question and mark your answer
- A if all the names are different
- B if only two names are exactly the same
- C if only three names are exactly the same
- D if all four names are exactly the same

EXAMPLE
Jensen, Alfred E.
Jensen, Alfred E.
Jensan, Alfred E.
Jensen, Fred E.

Since the name Jensen, Alfred E. appears twice and is exactly the same in both places, the correct answer is B.

1. A. Riviera, Pedro S. B. Rivers, Pedro S. 1.____
   C. Riviera, Pedro N. D. Riviera, Juan S.

2. A. Guider, Albert B. Guidar, Albert 2.____
   C. Giuder, Alfred D. Guider, Albert

3. A. Blum, Rona B. Blum, Rona 3.____
   C. Blum, Rona D. Blum, Rona

4. A. Raugh, John B. Raugh, James 4.____
   C. Raughe, John D. Raugh, John

5. A. Katz, Stanley B. Katz, Stanley 5.____
   C. Katze, Stanley D. Katz, Stanley

Questions 6-10.

DIRECTIONS: Each Question 6 through 10 consists of numbers or letters in Columns I and II. For each question, compare each line of Column I with its corresponding line in Column II and decide how many lines in Column I are EXACTLY the same as their corresponding lines in Column II. In your answer space, mark your answer
- A if only ONE line in Column I is exactly the same as its corresponding line in Column II
- B if only TWO lines in Column I are exactly the same as their corresponding lines in Column II

C if only THREE lines in Column I are exactly the same as their corresponding lines in Column II
D if all FOUR lines in Column I are exactly the same as their corresponding lines in Column II

EXAMPLE

Column I	Column II
1776	1776
1865	1865
1945	1945
1976	1978

Only three lines in Column I are exactly the same as their corresponding lines in Column II. Therefore, the correct answer is C.

	Column I	Column II	
6.	5653	5653	6.____
	8727	8728	
	ZPSS	ZPSS	
	4952	9453	
7.	PNJP	PNPJ	7.____
	NJPJ	NJPJ	
	JNPN	JNPN	
	PNJP	PNPJ	
8.	effe	eFfe	8.____
	uWvw	uWvw	
	KpGj	KpGg	
	vmnv	vmnv	
9.	5232	5232	9.____
	PfrC	PfrN	
	zssz	zzss	
	rwwr	rwww	
10.	czws	czws	10.____
	cecc	cece	
	thrm	thrm	
	lwtz	lwtz	

Questions 11-15.

DIRECTIONS: Questions 11 through 15 have lines of letters and numbers. Each letter should be matched with its number in accordance with the following table.

Letter	F	R	C	A	W	L	E	N	B	T
Matching Number	0	1	2	3	4	5	6	7	8	9

From the table you can determine that the letter F has the matching number 0 below it, the letter R has the matching number 1 below, etc.

For each question, compare each line of letters and numbers carefully to see if each letter has its correct matching number. If all the letters and numbers are matched correctly in

none of the lines of the question, mark your answer A
only *one* of the lines of the question, mark your answer B
only *two* of the lines of the question, mark your answer C
all three lines of the question, mark your answer D

EXAMPLE

WBCR	4826
TLBF	9580
ATNE	3986

There is a mistake in the first line because the letter R should have its matching number 1 instead of the number 6.

The second line is correct because each letter shown has the correct matching number.

There is a mistake in the third line because the letter N should have the matching number 7 instead of the number 8.

Since all the letters and numbers are correct matched in only one of the lines in the sample, the correct answer is B.

11. EBCT   6829   11._____
     ATWR   3961
     NLBW   7584

12. RNCT   1729   12._____
     LNCR   5728
     WAEB   5368

13. NTWB   7948   13._____
     RABL   1385
     TAEF   9360

14. LWRB   5417   14._____
     RLWN   1647
     CBWA   2843

15. ABTC   3792   15._____
     WCER   5261
     AWCN   3417

16. Your job often brings you into contact with the public. 16._____
    Of the following, it would be MOST desirable to explain the reasons for official actions to people coming into your office for assistance because such explanations
    A. help build greater understanding between the public and your agency
    B. help build greater self-confidence in city employees
    C. convince the public that nothing they do can upset a city employee
    D. show the public that city employees are intelligent

17. Assume that you strongly dislike one of your co-workers.
    You should FIRST
    A. discuss your feeling with the co-worker
    B. demand a transfer to another office
    C. suggest to your supervisor that the co-worker should be observed carefully
    D. try to figure out the reason for this dislike before you say or do anything

18. An office worker who has problems accepting authority is MOST likely to find it difficult to
    A. obey rules
    B. understand people
    C. assist other employees
    D. follow complex instructions

19. The employees in your office have taken a dislike to one person and frequently annoy her.
    Your supervisor should
    A. transfer this person to another unit at the first opportunity
    B. try to find out the reason for the staff's attitude before doing anything about it
    C. threaten to transfer the first person observed bothering this person
    D. ignore the situation

20. Assume that your supervisor has asked a worker in your office to get a copy of a report out of the files. You notice the worker as accidentally pulled out the wrong report.
    Of the following, the BEST way for you to handle this situation is to tell
    A. the worker about all the difficulties that will result from this error
    B. the worker about her mistake in a nice way
    C. the worker to ignore this error
    D. your supervisor that this worker needs more training in how to use the files

21. Filing systems differ in their efficiency.
    Which of the following is the BEST way to evaluate the efficiency of a filing system? A
    A. number of times used per day
    B. amount of material that is received each day for filing
    C. amount of time it takes to locate material
    D. type of locking system used

22. In planning ahead so that a sufficient amount of general office supplies is always available, it would be LEAST important to find out the
    A. current office supply needs of the staff
    B. amount of office supplies used last year
    C. days and times that office supplies can be ordered
    D. agency goals and objectives

23. The MAIN reason for establishing routine office work procedures is that once a routine is established
    A. work need not be checked for accuracy
    B. all steps in the routine will take an equal amount of time to perform
    C. each time the job is repeated, it will take less time to perform
    D. each step in the routine will not have to be planned all over again each time

24. When an office machine centrally located in an agency must be shut down for repairs, the bureaus and divisions using this machine should be informed of the
    A. expected length of time before the machine will be in operation again
    B. estimated cost of repairs
    C. efforts being made to avoid future repairs
    D. type of new equipment which the agency may buy in the future to replace the machine being repaired

25. If the day's work is properly scheduled, the MOST important result would be that the
    A. supervisor will not have to do much supervision
    B. employee will know what to do next
    C. employee will show greater initiative
    D. job will become routine

KEY (CORRECT ANSWERS)

1.	A		11.	C
2.	B		12.	B
3.	D		13.	D
4.	B		14.	B
5.	C		15.	A
6.	B		16.	A
7.	B		17.	D
8.	B		18.	A
9.	A		19.	B
10.	C		20.	B

21.	C
22.	D
23.	D
24.	A
25.	B

EXAMINATION SECTION

TEST 1

DIRECTIONS: Each question or incomplete statement is followed by several suggested answers or completions. Select the one that BEST answers the question or completes the statement. *PRINT THE LETTER OF THE CORRECT ANSWER IN THE SPACE AT THE RIGHT.*

1. Which one of the following is considered a word processor program?
   A. Microsoft Word
   B. Microsoft Works
   C. Notepad
   D. Both A and B

   1.____

2. Default headings are available under the _____ tab.
   A. Insert
   B. Home
   C. File
   D. View

   2.____

3. _____ deals with font, alignment and margins.
   A. Selecting
   B. Formatting
   C. Composing
   D. Pattern

   3.____

4. Which one of the following is the BEST format for storing bit-mapped images on the computer?
   A. .JPG
   B. .PNG
   C. .GIF
   D. .TIF

   4.____

5. A header specifies an area in the _____ margins of every page.
   A. top
   B. bottom
   C. left
   D. right

   5.____

6. When an Excel file is inserted into a Word document, the data is
   A. hyperlinked
   B. placed in a Word table
   C. linked
   D. embedded

   6.____

7. A workbook in Excel is a file that
   A. is primarily used to generate graphs
   B. is often used for word processing
   C. can contain many sheets, chart sheets and worksheets
   D. both A and B

   7.____

8. Excel can produce chart types that include
   A. only line graphs
   B. bar charts, line graphs and pie charts
   C. line graphs and pie charts only
   D. bar charts and line graphs only

   8.____

9. In PowerPoint, the motion path is a
   A. method of moving items on the slide
   B. method of advancing slides
   C. indentation
   D. type of animation

   9.____

10. _____ replaces similar words in a document.
    A. Word Count   B. Thesaurus   C. Wrap Text   D. Format Printer

11. The MOST simple description of the Internet is
    A. a single network
    B. a huge collection of different networks
    C. collection of LANs
    D. single WAN

12. How can a computer be connected to the Internet?
    A. Through internet service providers   B. Internet society
    C. Internet architecture board   D. Local area network

13. A software program that is used to view web pages is known as a(n)
    A. Internet browser   B. interpreter
    C. operating system   D. website

14. Which of the following is used to search anything on the Internet?
    A. Search engines   B. Routers
    C. Social networks   D. Websites

15. When a website is accessed, its main page is called
    A. home page   B. back end page
    C. dead end   D. both A and B

16. Google Docs provides _____, which is a salient feature of Google Doc.
    A. image processing   B. synchronization
    C. both A and B   D. installation

17. Documents in Google Drive could be accessed from
    A. only a personal computer
    B. any computer that has Internet connection
    C. only that computer that has Google drive on hard disk
    D. both B and C

18. In an email address, for example test@gmail.com, "gmail" is known as
    A. domain
    B. host computer in commercial domain
    C. internet service provider
    D. URL

19. Which of the following is NOT a well-known domain?
    A. .edu   B. .com   C. .org   D. .army

20. Cyberspace is an alternative name used for
    A. Internet   B. information   C. virtual space   D. data space

21. Which one of the following is NOT an Internet browser?
    A. Chrome   B. Firefly   C. Firefox   D. Safari

22. Which of the following is NOT a past or current search engine? 22.____
    A. Apple B. Lycos C. Bing D. Google

23. Document scanning could be done through 23.____
    A. OCR B. OMR
    C. both A and B D. dot-matrix printer

24. _____ are used to fill out empty fields in scanned images of data. 24.____
    A. Computerized optical scanners B. OCR software
    C. Scanners D. Laser printers

25. All of the following are examples of hardware for standard home use EXCEPT 25.____
    A. flash drives B. inkjet printers
    C. servers D. laser printers

KEY (CORRECT ANSWERS)

1. D
2. B
3. B
4. D
5. A

6. B
7. C
8. B
9. A
10. B

11. B
12. A
13. A
14. A
15. A

16. B
17. B
18. B
19. D
20. A

21. B
22. A
23. C
24. A
25. C

TEST 2

DIRECTIONS: Each question or incomplete statement is followed by several suggested answers or completions. Select the one that BEST answers the question or completes the statement. *PRINT THE LETTER OF THE CORRECT ANSWER IN THE SPACE AT THE RIGHT.*

1. In a spreadsheet, data is organized in the form of 1.____
   A. lines and spaces B. rows and columns
   C. layers and planes D. height and width

2. Which one of the following menus is used to protect a worksheet? 2.____
   A. Edit B. Format C. Data D. Tools

3. _____ corrects spelling mistakes automatically. 3.____
   A. Word wrap B. AutoCorrect
   C. Spell checker D. Thesaurus

4. Which function is used to automatically align text? 4.____
   A. Justification B. Indentation
   C. Both A and B D. None of the above

5. Orientation is the property of the _____ function. 5.____
   A. Print B. Design
   C. Image D. Both A and B

6. Special effects that are used to present slides in a presentation are known as 6.____
   A. effects B. custom animation
   C. transition D. present animation

7. Page setup and print functions can typically be found in the ____ menu. 7.____
   A. tools B. format C. file D. edit

8. Which one of the following is considered removable storage media? 8.____
   A. Scanner B. Flash drive
   C. External hard drive D. Both B and C

9. Which component of the computer is called the brain of the computer? 9.____
   A. ALU B. Memory C. Control Unit D. CPU

10. .txt is a file that is named for _____ files. 10.____
    A. Notepad B. Word C. Paint D. Excel

11. Software programs that are automatically downloaded and work within a browser are known as 11.____
    A. plug-in B. utilities C. widgets D. add-on

12. _____ is a computer that requests data from other computers on the Internet.
    A. Client B. Server C. Super computer D. Personal computer

13. A wizard is considered as a _____ file with prompt display.
    A. system B. program C. help D. application

14. E-mails from unknown senders go into the _____ folder.
    A. Spam B. Trash C. Drafts D. Inbox

15. LAN is an abbreviation for _____ area network.
    A. line B. local C. large D. limited

16. Which of the following is NOT an extension for an image file?
    A. .bmp B. .jpg C. .png D. .xls

17. In the e-mail address *test@gmail.com*, "test" is the _____ name.
    A. domain B. user C. server D. ISP

18. To e-mail multiple recipients while hiding the recipients from view, use the ___ function.
    A. BCC B. CC C. send D. hide

19. The system that translates an IP address into a simple form that is easy to remember is
    A. domain name system B. domain
    C. domain numbering system D. server domain

20. Which one of the following is the CORRECT method to send a file through e-mail?
    A. CC B. Attachment
    C. Embed through HTML D. Both A and B

21. Inkjet printers are categorized as a(n) _____ printer.
    A. character B. ink C. line D. band

22. Which one of the following is a storage medium that has a shape of a circular plate?
    A. Disk B. CPU C. ALU D. Printer

23. Ctrl+P activates the _____ function.
    A. reboot B. save C. print D. paint

24. The file extension .exe represents an _____ file.
    A. examination B. extra C. executable D. extension

25. Which of the following is NOT considered an input device?
    A. OCR
    B. Optical scanner
    C. Printer
    D. Keyboard

25._____

KEY (CORRECT ANSWERS)

1. B
2. D
3. B
4. A
5. A

6. C
7. C
8. D
9. D
10. A

11. B
12. A
13. C
14. A
15. B

16. D
17. B
18. A
19. A
20. B

21. C
22. A
23. C
24. C
25. C

TEST 3

DIRECTIONS: Each question or incomplete statement is followed by several suggested answers or completions. Select the one that BEST answers the question or completes the statement. *PRINT THE LETTER OF THE CORRECT ANSWER IN THE SPACE AT THE RIGHT.*

1. Excel is a _____ program. 1._____
   - A. graphics
   - B. word processor
   - C. spreadsheet
   - D. typewriter

2. Basically, a word processor program like Microsoft Word is a replacement for 2._____
   - A. manual work
   - B. typewriters
   - C. both A and B
   - D. graphical programs

3. Which one of the following could be added as a sound effect to a PowerPoint presentation? 3._____
   - A. .wav files and .mid files
   - B. .wav files and .gif files
   - C. .wav files and .jpg files
   - D. .jpg files and .gif files

4. Google Drive is an example of _____ software. 4._____
   - A. system   B. application   C. database   D. firmware

5. PDF stands for _____ document format. 5._____
   - A. portable   B. picture   C. plain   D. private

6. Which one of the following is an example of internal memory of a computer? 6._____
   - A. Disks   B. Pen drive   C. RAM   D. CDs

7. A keyboard is an example of a(n) _____ device. 7._____
   - A. input
   - B. output
   - C. word processor
   - D. printing

8. Clip art is a collection of _____ that can be inserted into a document. 8._____
   - A. text files
   - B. image files
   - C. templates
   - D. audio files

9. _____ is a distinctive part of memory which holds the contents temporarily during cut or copy functions. 9._____
   - A. Clipboard   B. Macro   C. Template   D. Clip art

10. _____ is a process to store files on a computer from the Internet. 10._____
    - A. Uploading
    - B. Downloading
    - C. Pulling
    - D. Transferring

11. "Cut and paste" refers to 11._____
    - A. deleting and moving text
    - B. restoring and updating software
    - C. cleaning images
    - D. replacing images

12. Which one of the following is a compressed format for images? 12.____
    A. GIF B. JPGE C. PNG D. JPG

13. A computer stores information and data inside the 13.____
    A. hard drive B. CPU C. CD D. monitor

14. WWW is an abbreviation of 14.____
    A. world wide web
    B. wide world web
    C. web worldwide
    D. world wide website

15. A _____ computer holds more than one processor. 15.____
    A. multithread
    B. multi-unit
    C. multiprocessor
    D. multiprogramming

16. Landscape and portrait are properties of 16.____
    A. page layout B. design C. formatting D. text

17. _____ includes the company's name, address, phone number and e-mail address. 17.____
    A. Letterhead B. Template C. Visiting Card D. Brochure

18. _____ Server provides database services for other computers. 18.____
    A. Application B. Web C. Database D. FTP

19. Which one of the following is responsible for storing movies, images and pictures? 19.____
    A. File server
    B. Web server
    C. Database server
    D. Application server

20. GUI stands for graphical 20.____
    A. user interface
    B. unified instrument
    C. unified interface
    D. user instrument

21. Scanner is an example of a(n) _____ device. 21.____
    A. output B. input C. printing D. both A and B

22. Which one of the following is NOT an example of computer hardware? 22.____
    A. Printer B. Scanner C. Mouse D. Antivirus

23. Which one of the following provides the BEST quality reproduction of graphics? 23.____
    A. Laser printer
    B. Inkjet printer
    C. Dot-matrix printer
    D. Plotter

24. If an e-mail sender is unknown, then do not download the _____ because it might contain a virus. 24.____
    A. attachment
    B. email
    C. spam
    D. both A and B

25. The BEST way to send identical emails to more than one person is to 25.____
    A. use the CC option B. add email ID to address
    C. forward D. both A and B

KEY (CORRECT ANSWERS)

1. C
2. B
3. A
4. B
5. A

6. C
7. A
8. B
9. A
10. B

11. A
12. A
13. A
14. A
15. C

16. A
17. A
18. C
19. A
20. A

21. B
22. D
23. D
24. A
25. A

TEST 4

DIRECTIONS: Each question or incomplete statement is followed by several suggested answers or completions. Select the one that BEST answers the question or completes the statement. *PRINT THE LETTER OF THE CORRECT ANSWER IN THE SPACE AT THE RIGHT.*

1. A keyboard shortcut for saving files is
   A. Alt+S   B. Ctrl+S   C. Ctrl+SV   D. S+Enter

2. Which of the following is NOT a term relevant to Excel?
   A. slide
   B. cell
   C. formula
   D. column

3. A _____ background is a grainy and non-smooth surface.
   A. texture   B. gradient   C. solid   D. pattern

4. Word wrap forces all text to fit within the defined
   A. margin   B. indent   C. block   D. box

5. In Microsoft Word, overview of the prepared document could be better seen through
   A. Preview
   B. Print Preview
   C. Review
   D. both A and B

6. The amount of vertical space between text line in a document is known as
   A. double space
   B. line spacing
   C. single space
   D. vertical spacing

7. Which one of the following devices is required for Internet connection?
   A. Joy stick   B. Modem   C. NIC card   D. Optical drive

8. IBM is a short form used for
   A. Internal Business Management
   B. International Business Management
   C. Internal Business Machines
   D. International Business Machines

9. Which one of the following is static and non-volatile memory?
   A. RAM   B. ROM   C. BIOS   D. Cache

10. One disadvantage of Google Docs is
    A. less storage
    B. compatibility
    C. needs connectivity to Internet
    D. synchronization

11. WAN is an abbreviation of _____ area network.
    A. wide   B. wired   C. whole   D. while

12. Bibliography can be created through the _____ tab.
    A. References   B. Design   C. Review   D. Insert

13. The _____ is MOST likely shared in a computer network.
    A. keyboard   B. speaker   C. printer   D. scanner

14. A normal computer is not able to boot if it does not have a(n)
    A. operating system
    B. complier
    C. loader
    D. assembler

15. _____ is another name for junk e-mails.
    A. Spam   B. Spoof   C. Spool   D. Sniffer scripts

16. A table of contents can be created automatically by using an option in
    A. Page Layout   B. Insert   C. References   D. View

17. ALU stands for
    A. arithmetic logic unit
    B. array logic unit
    C. application logic unit
    D. both A and B

18. Orientation is concerned with the _____ set-up of the page.
    A. horizontal   B. vertical   C. both A and B   D. spacing

19. _____ is a form of written communication within the same company which comprises guide words as heading.
    A. Memorandum
    B. Letterhead
    C. Template
    D. None of the above

20. Which one of the following is NOT a web browser?
    A. Chrome   B. Opera   C. Firefox   D. Drupal

21. .net domain is specifically used for
    A. international organization
    B. internet infrastructure and service providers
    C. educational institutes
    D. commercial business

22. A modem is not required when the Internet is connected through
    A. Wi-Fi
    B. LAN
    C. dial-up phone
    D. cable

23. Mail Merge uses _____ to create separate copies of a document for multiple people in Microsoft Word.
    A. primary document
    B. data document
    C. both A and B
    D. web page

24. Linux is an example of
    A. operating system
    B. malware
    C. firmware
    D. application program

25. Which one of the following is a CORRECT format for a website address? 25._____
    A. www@com
    B. www.test.com
    C. www.test25A@com
    D. www#TeST.com

KEY (CORRECT ANSWERS)

1.	B	11.	A
2.	A	12.	A
3.	B	13.	C
4.	A	14.	A
5.	B	15.	A
6.	B	16.	C
7.	B	17.	A
8.	D	18.	C
9.	B	19.	A
10.	C	20.	D

21. B
22. A
23. C
24. A
25. B

EXAMINATION SECTION

TEST 1

DIRECTIONS: Each question or incomplete statement is followed by several suggested answers or completions. Select the one that BEST answers the question or completes the statement. *PRINT THE LETTER OF THE CORRECT ANSWER IN THE SPACE AT THE RIGHT.*

1. Physical components of computers are known as 1.____
   A. software B. hardware C. firmware D. human ware

2. A touchscreen is considered a(n) _____ device. 2.____
   A. input B. output C. display D. both A and B

3. Keyboards and microphones are examples of computer 3.____
   A. peripherals B. software C. add-ons D. uploads

4. Unauthorized access to a computer is prevented through the use of 4.____
   A. passwords B. user logins
   C. access control software D. computer keys

5. In order to establish an Internet connection, a modem is always connected to a 5.____
   A. keyboard B. monitor
   C. telephone line D. printer

6. _____ does NOT hold data permanently. 6.____
   A. RAM B. ROM C. Hard drive D. Flash drive

7. Identification of a user who comes back to the same website is done through the use of 7.____
   A. scripts B. plug-in C. cookies D. both A and B

8. File _____ is the process of moving a file from one computer to another computer across the network. 8.____
   A. encryption B. transfer C. copying D. updating

9. _____ is a type of software that controls specific hardware. 9.____
   A. Driver B. Browser C. Plug-in D. Control panel

10. _____ is a downloadable program that is used for Internet surfing. 10.____
    A. Messenger B. Firefox
    C. Windows Explorer D. Internet

11. In Microsoft Word, _____ is NOT a font style. 11.____
    A. Bold B. Regular C. Superscript D. Italic

12. Which of the following is NOT associated with page margins in a Word document?   12._____
    A. Top   B. Center   C. Left   D. Right

13. Microsoft Office is a type of _____ software.   13._____
    A. application   B. system   C. Internet   D. website

14. A function that is inside another function is known as a(n) _____ function.   14._____
    A. round   B. nested   C. sum   D. average

15. To write a formula in Microsoft Excel, a user would start by typing   15._____
    A. %   B. =   C. #   D. @

16. The individual boxes used for data entry in an Excel file are known as   16._____
    A. cells   B. data points
    C. formulas   D. squares

17. In PowerPoint, _____ do NOT show with the slide layout.   17._____
    A. titles   B. animations   C. lists   D. charts

18. _____ is a basic option when looking for colorful images or graphics to publish   18._____
    in a PowerPoint presentation.
    A. Clip art   B. Online search
    C. MS Paint   D. Drawing

19. In a web browser, the addresses of Internet pages are known as   19._____
    A. web pages   B. URLs   C. scripts   D. plug-in

20. A company that provides Internet services is called a(n)   20._____
    A. ISP   B. IBM   C. LAN   D. Both A and B

21. _____ is the process of copying a file from personal computer to a remote   21._____
    computer.
    A. Downloading   B. Uploading
    C. Updating   D. Modification

22. _____ is a text that opens another page when clicked.   22._____
    A. Link   B. Hyperlink
    C. Both A and B   D. Web page

23. Dots per inch is the measure of printing   23._____
    A. quality   B. type   C. time   D. layout

24. _____ is the collection of computers connected with each other.   24._____
    A. Group   B. Team   C. Network   D. Meeting

25. Which one of the following is considered a high-end printer?   25._____
    A. Dot matrix printer   B. Inkjet printer
    C. Laser   D. Thermal

KEY (CORRECT ANSWERS)

1. B
2. D
3. A
4. A
5. C

6. A
7. C
8. B
9. A
10. B

11. C
12. B
13. A
14. B
15. B

16. A
17. B
18. A
19. B
20. A

21. B
22. C
23. A
24. C
25. C

TEST 2

DIRECTIONS: Each question or incomplete statement is followed by several suggested answers or completions. Select the one that BEST answers the question or completes the statement. *PRINT THE LETTER OF THE CORRECT ANSWER IN THE SPACE AT THE RIGHT.*

1. Which one of the following is a storage device? 1.____
   A. Printer
   B. Hard drive
   C. Scanner
   D. Motherboard

2. DVD is an example of a(n) _____ disk. 2.____
   A. hard
   B. optical
   C. magnetic
   D. floppy

3. _____ computers provide resources to other computers across the network. 3.____
   A. Server
   B. Client
   C. Framework
   D. Digital

4. Random access memory is considered _____ computer memory. 4.____
   A. non-volatile
   B. volatile
   C. cache
   D. permanent

5. Which one of the following is NOT an operating system? 5.____
   A. Windows
   B. IOS
   C. Android
   D. MS Office

6. A(n) _____ is a person who gets illegal access to a computer system and steals information. 6.____
   A. administrator
   B. computer operator
   C. hacker
   D. programmer

7. Which one of the following is NOT application software? 7.____
   A. MS Word
   B. Media player
   C. Linux
   D. MS Power Point

8. Which one of the following represents a domain name? 8.____
   A. .com
   B. www
   C. URL
   D. HTTP

9. _____ is NOT an example of an Internet browser. 9.____
   A. Opera
   B. Google
   C. Mozilla
   D. Internet Explorer

10. Which one of the following is/was NOT a search engine? 10.____
    A. Altavista
    B. Bing
    C. Yahoo
    D. Facebook

11. E-mail is an abbreviation of 11.____
    A. electronic mail
    B. easy mail
    C. electric email
    D. both A and B

12. A(n) _____ is a person who takes care of websites for large companies. 12.____
    A. administrator B. webmaster
    C. programmer D. hacker

13. _____ connect web pages with each other. 13.____
    A. Connecters B. Links C. Hyperlinks D. Browsers

14. _____ is a program that is harmful for computers. 14.____
    A. Spam B. Virus
    C. Operating system D. Plug-in

15. CC is an abbreviation of _____ in emails. 15.____
    A. core copy B. copycat
    C. carbon copy D. copy copy

16. Software most commonly used for basic personal computing is 16.____
    A. Excel B. SPSS C. Illustrator D. Dreamweaver

17. _____ is an option to send the same letter to different persons. 17.____
    A. Template B. Macros C. Mail Merge D. Layout

18. Which one of the following is a file extension for MS Word? 18.____
    A. .doc B. .txt C. .bmp D. .pdf

19. _____ displays the number of words in a document. 19.____
    A. Character Count B. Word Count C. Word Wrap D. Thesaurus

20. In an Excel sheet, an active cell is specified with 20.____
    A. dotted border B. dark wide border
    C. italic text D. a dotted border

21. A(n) _____ is a file that contains rows and columns. 21.____
    A. database B. spreadsheet
    C. word D. drawing

22. _____ are objects on the slides that hold text in a PowerPoint presentation. 22.____
    A. Placeholders B. Text holders
    C. Auto layouts D. Object holders

23. Which one of the following brings up the first slide in a PowerPoint presentation? 23.____
    A. Ctrl+End B. Ctrl+Home
    C. Page up D. Next slide button

24. Which one of the following sends printing commands to a printer? 24.____
    A. F5 B. Ctrl+P C. Ctrl+S D. F12

25. Scanners are used to capture _____ copy of documents. 25.____
    A. soft B. hard C. single D. first

KEY (CORRECT ANSWERS)

1.	B	11.	A
2.	B	12.	B
3.	A	13.	C
4.	B	14.	B
5.	D	15.	C
6.	C	16.	A
7.	C	17.	C
8.	A	18.	A
9.	B	19.	B
10.	D	20.	B

21. B
22. A
23. B
24. B
25. B

TEST 3

DIRECTIONS: Each question or incomplete statement is followed by several suggested answers or completions. Select the one that BEST answers the question or completes the statement. *PRINT THE LETTER OF THE CORRECT ANSWER IN THE SPACE AT THE RIGHT.*

1. Which one of the following is the MOST appropriate operation to move a text block in MS Word?
   A. Cut
   B. Save As
   C. Cut and Paste
   D. Copy and Paste
   1.____

2. The Navigation pane opens under the _____ tab.
   A. View B. Review C. Page Layout D. Mailings
   2.____

3. Ctrl+B makes selected test
   A. italic B. bold C. bigger D. uppercase
   3.____

4. _____ is NOT an acceptable formula in Excel.
   A. 10+50 B. =10+50 C. =B7+B8 D. =B7*B8
   4.____

5. A worksheet usually contains _____ columns.
   A. 128 B. 256 C. 512 D. 320
   5.____

6. _____ is the process of getting data from the cell that is located in different worksheets.
   A. Accessing B. Referencing C. Updating D. Functioning
   6.____

7. The shortcut _____ selects all PowerPoint slides at once.
   A. Ctrl+Home B. Ctrl+A C. Alt+Home D. Shift+A
   7.____

8. By pressing Ctrl+V in a Word document, the user
   A. pastes text
   B. cuts and pastes text
   C. adds a video box
   D. deletes a page
   8.____

9. Transitions are applicable only on
   A. Excel worksheets
   B. PowerPoint slides
   C. image files
   D. Word document
   9.____

10. In MS Word, the _____ tab has options for margin, orientation and spacing.
    A. Design B. Review C. Page Layout D. Insert
    10.____

11. Which one of the following is graphic software?
    A. MS Office
    B. Adobe Photoshop
    C. Firefox
    D. Notepad
    11.____

12. Which one of the following is a social networking website?
    A. Facebook B. Yahoo C. Google D. ASK
    12.____

111

13. A computer monitor is referred to as a(n) _____ device.   13._____
    A. output   B. input   C. sound   D. printing

14. _____ memory is another name for the main memory of the computer.   14._____
    A. Primary   B. Direct   C. Simple   D. Quick

15. An operating system is _____ software.   15._____
    A. application   B. system   C. editing   D. both A and C

16. Which one of the following pieces of equipment is necessary for video calls?   16._____
    A. Webcam   B. Mouse   C. Scanner   D. Printer

17. _____ is a primary input device that is used to enter text and numbers.   17._____
    A. Mouse   B. Keyboard   C. Joystick   D. Microphone

18. Of the following, which is NOT an example of a web browser?   18._____
    A. Firefox   B. Opera   C. Chrome   D. Google Talk

19. A _____ is a collection of many web pages that are related to each other.   19._____
    A. web browser   B. website
    C. search engine   D. Firefox

20. Which one of the following is considered a personal journal used for posts?   20._____
    A. Blog   B. E-mail   C. Chat   D. Messengers

21. Windows _____ provides security against external threats.   21._____
    A. antivirus   B. spyware   C. firmware   D. firewall

22. Desktop and laptop computers are different from each other in terms of _____ and cost.   22._____
    A. operating system   B. functions
    C. physical structure   D. application software

23. _____ is a process of stealing confidential information without permission of the user.   23._____
    A. Forwarding   B. Hacking   C. Searching   D. Complaining

24. RAM is located in the _____ board.   24._____
    A. extension   B. external   C. mother   D. chip

25. All files on the computer are stored in   25._____
    A. hard drive   B. RAM
    C. cache   D. associative memory

KEY (CORRECT ANSWERS)

1. C
2. A
3. B
4. A
5. B

6. B
7. B
8. A
9. B
10. C

11. B
12. A
13. A
14. A
15. B

16. A
17. B
18. D
19. B
20. A

21. D
22. C
23. B
24. C
25. A

TEST 4

DIRECTIONS: Each question or incomplete statement is followed by several suggested answers or completions. Select the one that BEST answers the question or completes the statement. *PRINT THE LETTER OF THE CORRECT ANSWER IN THE SPACE AT THE RIGHT.*

1. Which one of the following functions are performed by RAM?
   A. Read and Write
   B. Read
   C. Write
   D. Update

2. _____ is an example of secondary storage.
   A. Diode
   B. Hard disk
   C. RAM
   D. ROM

3. USB is a type of _____ storage.
   A. primary
   B. secondary
   C. tertiary
   D. temporary

4. MPG file extension is used for _____ files.
   A. video
   B. audio
   C. image
   D. flash

5. .exe is an extension for _____ files.
   A. saved
   B. executable
   C. system
   D. software

6. Which one of the following is NOT a type of printer?
   A. Inkjet
   B. Dot matrix
   C. Laser
   D. CRT

7. _____ sends digital data across a phone line.
   A. Flash
   B. Modem
   C. NIC card
   D. Keyboard

8. _____ is a wireless technology used to transfer data among devices over short distances.
   A. USB
   B. Modem
   C. Wi-Fi
   D. Bluetooth

9. A user is listening to a song on his computer's music player. He is most likely listening to a(n) _____ file.
   A. .exe
   B. .mus
   C. .wav
   D. .mp3

10. PNG is an extension used for _____ files.
    A. audio
    B. video
    C. text
    D. image

11. Cache memory is located in the
    A. monitor
    B. CPU
    C. DVD
    D. hard drive

12. Computer resolution determines the number of
    A. colors
    B. pixels
    C. images
    D. icons

13. _____ is an extension used for images.
    A. GIF
    B. MP3
    C. MPG
    D. PPT

14. Which one of the following is NOT an e-mail server? 14.____
    A. Gmail   B. Yahoo   C. Chrome   D. Hotmail

15. _____ is an operating system developed by Apple. 15.____
    A. Mac IOS   B. Linux   C. Android   D. Windows

16. "What You See Is What You Get" (WYSIWYG) refers to 16.____
    A. editing text and graphics for web design
    B. buying a computer at a set price that can't be negotiated
    C. purchasing products as is on websites like Amazon and eBay
    D. printing web pages exactly as they appear on the screen

17. Which one of the following is the BEST option to add a new slide in an existing PowerPoint presentation? 17.____
    A. File, add a new slide   B. File, open
    C. Insert, new slide   D. File, new

18. _____ is the default setup for page orientation in PowerPoint. 18.____
    A. Horizontal B. Vertical   C. Landscape   D. Portrait

19. Items in a list are typically shown by using 19.____
    A. graphics   B. bullets   C. icons   D. markers

20. In PowerPoint, _____ displays only text. 20.____
    A. outline view   B. slide show
    C. print view   D. slider sorter view

21. In Excel, a cell can be edited by use of 21.____
    A. a single click   B. a double click
    C. the format menu   D. formulas

22. Formulas are important features of Microsoft 22.____
    A. Word   B. PowerPoint C. Excel   D. Publisher

23. In MS Word, which one of the following is used to underline a text? 23.____
    A. Ctrl+I   B. Ctrl+B   C. Ctrl+U   D. Ctrl+P

24. Page color option can be found under the _____ tab. 24.____
    A. Page Layout B. Design   C. Insert   D. View

25. The F1 key typically displays a program's _____ menu. 25.____
    A. print   B. help
    C. tools   D. task manager

KEY (CORRECT ANSWERS)

1.	A		11.	B
2.	B		12.	B
3.	C		13.	A
4.	A		14.	C
5.	B		15.	A
6.	D		16.	A
7.	B		17.	C
8.	D		18.	C
9.	D		19.	B
10.	D		20.	A

21. A
22. C
23. C
24. B
25. B

CLERICAL ABILITIES
EXAMINATION SECTION
TEST 1

DIRECTIONS: Each question or incomplete statement is followed by several suggested answers or completions. Select the one that BEST answers the question or completes the statement. *PRINT THE LETTER OF THE CORRECT ANSWER IN THE SPACE AT THE RIGHT.*

Questions 1-4.

DIRECTIONS: Questions 1 through 4 are to be answered on the basis of the information given below.

The most commonly used filing system and the one that is easiest to learn is alphabetical filing. This involves putting records in an A to Z order, according to the letters of the alphabet. The name of a person is filed by using the following order: first, the surname or last name; second, the first name; third, the middle name or middle initial. For example, *Henry C. Young* is filed under *Y* and thereafter under *Young, Henry C.* The name of a company is filed in the same way. For example, *Long Cabinet Co.* is filed under *L* while *John T. Long Cabinet Co.* is filed under *L* and thereafter under *Long, John T. Cabinet Co.*

1. The one of the following which lists the names of persons in the CORRECT alphabetical order is:
   A. Mary Carrie, Helen Carrol, James Carson, John Carter
   B. James Carson, Mary Carrie, John Carter, Helen Carrol
   C. Helen Carrol, James Carson, John Carter, Mary Carrie
   D. John Carter, Helen Carrol, Mary Carrie, James Carson

1.____

2. The one of the following which lists the names of persons in the CORRECT alphabetical order is:
   A. Jones, John C.; Jones, John A.; Jones, John P.; Jones, John K.
   B. Jones, John P.; Jones, John K.; Jones, John C.; Jones, John A.
   C. Jones, John A.; Jones, John C.; Jones, John K.; Jones, John P.
   D. Jones, John K.; Jones, John C.; Jones, John A.; Jones, John P.

2.____

3. The one of the following which lists the names of the companies in the CORRECT alphabetical order is:
   A. Blane Co., Blake Co., Block Co., Blear Co.
   B. Blake Co., Blane Co., Blear Co., Block Co.
   C. Block Co., Blear Co., Blane Co., Blake Co.
   D. Blear Co., Blake Co., Blane Co., Block Co.

3.____

4. You are to return to the file an index card on *Barry C. Wayne Materials and Supplies Co.*
Of the following, the CORRECT alphabetical group that you should return the index card to is
   A. A to G B. H to M C. N to S D. T to Z

4._____

Questions 5-10.

DIRECTIONS: In each of Questions 5 through 10, the names of four people are given. For each question, choose as your answer the one of the four names given which should be filed FIRST according to the usual system of alphabetical filing of names, as described in the following paragraph.

In filing names, you must start with the last name. Names are filed in order of the first letter of the last name, then the second letter, etc. Therefore, BAILY would be filed before BROWN, which would be filed before COLT. A name with fewer letters of the same type comes first, i.e., Smith before Smithe. If the last names are the same, the names are filed alphabetically by the first name. If the first name is an initial, a name with an initial would come before a first name that starts with the same letter as the initial. Therefore, I. BROWN would come before IRA BROWN. Finally, if both last name and first name are the same, the name would be filed alphabetically by the middle name, once again an initial coming before a middle name which starts with the same letter as the initial. If there is no middle name at all, the name would come before those with middle initials or names.

SAMPLE QUESTION: A. Lester Daniels
B. William Dancer
C. Nathan Danzig
D. Dan Lester

The last names beginning with D are filed before the last name beginning with L. Since DANIELS, DANCER, and DANZIG all begin with the same three letters, you must look at the fourth letter of the last name to determine which name should be filed first. C comes before I or Z in the alphabet, so DANCER is filed before DANIELS or DANZIG. Therefore, the answer to the above sample question is B.

5. A. Scott Biala
   B. Mary Byala
   C. Martin Baylor
   D. Francis Bauer

5._____

6. A. Howard J. Black
   B. Howard Black
   C. J. Howard Black
   D. John H. Black

6._____

7. A. Theodora Garth Kingston
   B. Theadore Barth Kingston
   C. Thomas Kingston
   D. Thomas T. Kingston

7._____

8. A. Paulette Mary Huerta
    B. Paul M. Huerta
    C. Paulette L. Huerta
    D. Peter A. Huerta

9. A. Martha Hunt Morgan
    B. Martin Hunt Morgan
    C. Mary H. Morgan
    D. Martine H. Morgan

10. A. James T. Meerschaum
    B. James M. Mershum
    C. James F. Mearshaum
    D. James N. Meshum

Questions 11-14.

DIRECTIONS: Questions 11 through 14 are to be answered SOLELY on the basis of the following information.

You are required to file various documents in file drawers which are labeled according to the following pattern:

DOCUMENTS

MEMOS		LETTERS	
File	Subject	File	Subject
84PM1	(A-L)	84PC1	(A-L)
84PM2	(M-Z)	84PC2	(M-Z)

REPORTS		INQUIRIES	
File	Subject	File	Subject
84PR1	(A-L)	84PQ1	(A-L)
84PR2	(M-Z)	84PQ2	(M-Z)

11. A letter dealing with a burglary should be filed in the drawer labeled
    A. 84PM1   B. 84PC1   C. 84PR1   D. 84PQ2

12. A report on Statistics should be found in the drawer labeled
    A. 84PM1   B. 84PC2   C. 84PR2   D. 84PQS

13. An inquiry is received about parade permit procedures. It should be filed in the drawer labeled
    A. 84PM2   B. 84PC1   C. 84PR1   D. 84PQ2

14. A police officer has a question about a robbery report you filed. You should pull this file from the drawer labeled
    A. 84PM1   B. 84PM2   C. 84PR1   D. 84PR2

Questions 15-22.

DIRECTIONS: Each of Questions 15 through 22 consists of four or six numbered names. For each question, choose the option (A, B, C, or D) which indicates the order in which the names should be filed in accordance with the following filing instructions:
- File alphabetically according to last name, then first name, then middle initial.
- File according to each successive letter within a name.
- When comparing two names in which the letters in the longer name are identical to the corresponding letters in the shorter name, the shorter name is filed first.
- When the last names are the same, initials are always filed before names beginning with the same letter.

15. I. Ralph Robinson
    II. Alfred Ross
    III. Luis Robles
    IV. James Roberts

    The CORRECT filing sequence for the above names should be
    A. IV, II, I, III   B. I, IV, III, II   C. III, IV, I, II   D. IV, I, III, II

16. I. Irwin Goodwin
    II. Inez Gonzalez
    III. Irene Goodman
    IV. Ira S. Goodwin
    V. Ruth I. Goldstein
    VI. M.B. Goodman

    The CORRECT filing sequence for the above names should be
    A. V, II, I, IV, III, VI
    B. V, II, VI, III, IV, I
    C. V, II, III, VI, IV, I
    D. V, II, III, VI, I, IV

17. I. George Allan
    II. Gregory Allen
    III. Gary Allen
    IV. George Allen

    The CORRECT filing sequence for the above names should be
    A. IV, III, I, II   B. I, IV, II, III   C. III, IV, I, II   D. I, III, IV, II

18. I.   Simon Kauffman
     II. Leo Kaufman
     III. Robert Kaufmann
     IV. Paul Kauffmann

     The CORRECT filing sequence for the above names should be
     A. I, IV, II, III   B. II, IV, III, I   C. III, II, IV, I   D. I, II, III, IV

19. I.   Roberta Williams
     II. Robin Wilson
     III. Roberta Wilson
     IV. Robin Williams

     The CORRECT filing sequence for the above names should be
     A. III, II, IV, I   B. I, IV, III, II   C. I, II, III, IV   D. III, I, II, IV

20. I.   Lawrence Shultz
     II. Albert Schultz
     III. Theodore Schwartz
     IV. Thomas Schwarz
     V.   Alvin Schultz
     VI. Leonard Shultz

     The CORRECT filing sequence for the above names should be
     A. II, V, III, IV, I, VI   B. IV, III, V, I, II, VI
     C. II, V, I, VI, III, IV   D. I, VI, II, V, III, IV

21. I.   McArdle
     II. Mayer
     III. Maletz
     IV. McNiff
     V.   Meyer
     VI. MacMahon

     The CORRECT filing sequence for the above names should be
     A. I, IV, VI, III, II, V   B. II, I, IV, VI, III, V
     C. VI, III, II, I, IV, V   D. VI, III, II, V, I, IV

22. I.   Jack E. Johnson
     II. R.H. Jackson
     III. Bertha Jackson
     IV. J.T. Johnson
     V.   Ann Johns
     VI. John Jacobs

     The CORRECT filing sequence for the above names should be
     A. II, III, VI, V, IV, I   B. III, II, VI, V, IV, I
     C. VI, II, III, I, V, IV   D. III, II, VI, IV, V, I

Questions 23-30.

DIRECTIONS: The code table below shows 10 letters with matching numbers. For each question, there are three sets of letters. Each set of letters is followed by a set of numbers which may or may not match their correct letter according to the code table. For each question, check all three sets of letters and numbers and mark your answer:
- A. if no pairs are correctly matched
- B. if only one pair is correctly matched
- C. if only two pairs are correctly matched
- D. if all three pairs are correctly matched

CODE TABLE

T	M	V	D	S	P	R	G	B	H
1	2	3	4	5	6	7	8	9	0

SAMPLE QUESTION: TMVDSP – 123456
RGBHTM – 789011
DSPRGB – 256789

In the sample question above, the first set of numbers correctly match its set of letters. But the second and third pairs contain mistakes. In the second pair, M is correctly matched with number 1. According to the code table, letter M should be correctly matched with number 2. In the third pair, the letter D is incorrectly matched with number 2. According to the code table, letter D should be correctly matched with number 4. Since only one of the pairs is correctly matched, the answer to this sample question is B.

23. RSBMRM – 759262
    GDSRVH – 845730
    VDBRTM - 349713   23.____

24. TGVSDR – 183247
    SMHRDP – 520647
    TRMHSR - 172057   24.____

25. DSPRGM – 456782
    MVDBHT – 234902
    HPMDBT - 062491   25.____

26. BVPTRD – 936184
    GDPHMB – 807029
    GMRHMV - 827032   26.____

27. MGVRSH – 283750
    TRDMBS – 174295
    SPRMGV - 567283   27.____

28. SGBSDM – 489542
    MGHPTM – 290612
    MPBMHT - 269301

29. TDPBHM – 146902
    VPBMRS – 369275
    GDMBHM - 842902

30. MVPTBV – 236194
    PDRTMB – 47128
    BGTMSM - 981232

28.____

29.____

30.____

KEY (CORRECT ANSWERS)

1.	A	11.	B	21.	C		
2.	C	12.	C	22.	B		
3.	B	13.	D	23.	B		
4.	D	14.	D	24.	B		
5.	D	15.	D	25.	C		
6.	B	16.	C	26.	A		
7.	B	17.	D	27.	D		
8.	B	18.	A	28.	A		
9.	A	19.	B	29.	D		
10.	C	20.	A	30.	A		

TEST 2

DIRECTIONS: Each question or incomplete statement is followed by several suggested answers or completions. Select the one that BEST answers the question or completes the statement. *PRINT THE LETTER OF THE CORRECT ANSWER IN THE SPACE AT THE RIGHT.*

Questions 1-10.

DIRECTIONS: Questions 1 through 10 each consists of two columns, each containing four lines of names, numbers and/or addresses. For each question, compare the lines in Column I with the lines in Column II to see if they match exactly, and mark your answer A, B, C, or D, according to the following instructions:
- A. all four lines match exactly
- B. only three lines match exactly
- C. only two lines match exactly
- D. only one line matches exactly

	COLUMN I	COLUMN II	
1.	I. Earl Hodgson II. 1409870 III. Shore Ave. IV. Macon Rd.	Earl Hodgson 1408970 Schore Ave. Macon Rd.	1.____
2.	I. 9671485 II. 470 Astor Court III. Halprin, Phillip IV. Frank D. Poliseo	9671485 470 Astor Court Halperin, Phillip Frank D. Poliseo	2.____
3.	I. Tandem Associates II. 144-17 Northern Blvd. III. Alberta Forchi IV. Kings Park, NY 10751	Tandom Associates 144-17 Northern Blvd. Albert Forchi Kings Point, NY 10751	3.____
4.	I. Bertha C. McCormack II. Clayton, MO III. 976-4242 IV. New City, NY 10951	Bertha C. McCormack Clayton, MO 976-4242 New City, NY 10951	4.____
5.	I. George C. Morill II. Columbia, SC 29201 III. Louis Ingham IV. 3406 Forest Ave.	George C. Morrill Columbia, SD 29201 Louis Ingham 3406 Forest Ave.	5.____
6.	I. 506 S. Elliott Pl. II. Herbert Hall III. 4712 Rockaway Pkway IV. 169 E. 7 St.	506 S. Elliott Pl. Hurbert Hall 4712 Rockaway Pkway 169 E. 7 St.	6.____

7. I.   345 Park Ave.   345 Park Pl.   7._____
    II. Colman Oven Corp.   Coleman Oven Corp.
    III. Robert Conte   Robert Conti
    IV. 6179846   6179846

8. I.   Grigori Schierber   Grigori Schierber   8._____
    II. Des Moines, Iowa   Des Moines, Iowa
    III. Gouverneur Hospital   Gouverneur Hospital
    IV. 91-35 Cresskill Pl.   91-35 Cresskill Pl.

9. I.   Jeffery Janssen   Jeffrey Janssen   9._____
    II. 8041071   8041071
    III. 40 Rockefeller Plaza   40 Rockafeller Plaza
    IV. 407 6 St.   406 7 St.

10. I.   5971996   5871996   10._____
    II. 3113 Knickerbocker Ave.   31123 Knickerbocker Ave.
    III. 8434 Boston Post Rd.   8424 Boston Post Rd.
    IV. Penn Station   Penn Station

Questions 11-14.

DIRECTIONS: Questions 11 through 14 are to be answered by looking at the four groups of names and addresses listed below (I, II, III, and IV), and then finding out the number of groups that have their corresponding numbered lies exactly the same.

         GROUP I   GROUP II
Line 1. Richmond General Hospital   Richman General Hospital
Line 2. Geriatric Clinic   Geriatric Clinic
Line 3. 3975 Paerdegat St.   3975 Peardegat St.
Line 4. Loudonville, New York 11538   Londonville, New York 11538

         GROUP III   GROUP IV
Line 1. Richmond General Hospital   Richmend General Hospital
Line 2. Geriatric Clinic   Geriatric Clinic
Line 3. 3795 Paerdegat St.   3975 Paerdegat St.
Line 4. Loudonville, New York 11358   Loudonville, New York 11538

1. In how many groups is line one exactly the same?   11._____
       A. Two   B. Three   C. Four   D. None

12. In how many groups is line two exactly the same?   12._____
       A. Two   B. Three   C. Four   D. None

13. In how many groups is line three exactly the same?   13._____
       A. Two   B. Three   C. Four   D. None

3 (#2)

14. In how many groups is line four exactly the same? 14._____
    A. Two   B. Three   C. Four   D. None

Questions 15-18.

DIRECTIONS: Each of Questions 15 through 18 has two lists of names and addresses. Each list contains three sets of names and addresses. Check each of the three sets in the list on the right to see if they are the same as the corresponding set in the list on the left. Mark your answers:
    A. if none of the sets in the right list are the same as those in the left list
    B. if only one of the sets in the right list is the same as those in the left list
    C. if only two of the sets in the right list are the same as those in the left list
    D. if all three sets in the right list are the same as those in the left list

15. Mary T. Berlinger   Mary T. Berlinger   15._____
    2351 Hampton St.   2351 Hampton St.
    Monsey, N.Y. 20117   Monsey, N.Y. 20117

    Eduardo Benes   Eduardo Benes
    483 Kingston Avenue   473 Kingston Avenue
    Central Islip, N.Y. 11734   Central Islip, N.Y. 11734

    Alan Carrington Fuchs   Alan Carrington Fuchs
    17 Gnarled Hollow Road   17 Gnarled Hollow Road
    Los Angeles, CA 91635   Los Angeles, CA 91685

16. David John Jacobson   David John Jacobson   16._____
    178 34 St. Apt. 4C   178 53 St. Apt. 4C
    New York, N.Y. 00927   New York, N.Y. 00927

    Ann-Marie Calonella   Ann-Marie Calonella
    7243 South Ridge Blvd.   7243 South Ridge Blvd.
    Bakersfield, CA 96714   Bakersfield, CA 96714

    Pauline M. Thompson   Pauline M. Thomson
    872 Linden Ave.   872 Linden Ave.
    Houston, Texas 70321   Houston, Texas 70321

17. Chester LeRoy Masterton   Chester LeRoy Masterson   17._____
    152 Lacy Rd.   152 Lacy Rd.
    Kankakee, Ill. 54532   Kankakee, Ill. 54532

    William Maloney   William Maloney
    S. LaCrosse Pla.   S. LaCross Pla.
    Wausau, Wisconsin 52136   Wausau, Wisconsin 52146

    Cynthia V. Barnes   Cynthia V. Barnes
    16 Pines Rd.   16 Pines Rd.
    Greenpoint, Miss. 20376   Greenpoint,, Miss. 20376

18. Marcel Jean Frontenac   Marcel Jean Frontenac   18.____
     8 Burton On The Water   6 Burton On The Water
     Calender, Me. 01471   Calender, Me. 01471

     J. Scott Marsden   J. Scott Marsden
     174 S. Tipton St.   174 Tipton St.
     Cleveland, Ohio   Cleveland, Ohio

     Lawrence T. Haney   Lawrence T. Haney
     171 McDonough St.   171 McDonough St.
     Decatur, Ga. 31304   Decatur, Ga. 31304

Questions 19-26.

DIRECTIONS: Each of Questions 19 through 26 has two lists of numbers. Each list contains three sets of numbers. Check each of the three sets in the list on the right to see if they are the same as the corresponding set in the list on the left. Mark your answers:
  A. if none of the sets in the right list are the same as those in the left list
  B. if only one of the sets in the right list is the same as those in the left list
  C. if only two of the sets in the right list are the same as those in the left list
  D. if all three sets in the right list are the same as those in the left lists

19. 7354183476   7354983476   19.____
     4474747744   4474747774
     5791430231   57914302311

20. 7143592185   7143892185   20.____
     8344517699   8344518699
     9178531263   9178531263

21. 2572114731   257214731   21.____
     8806835476   8806835476
     8255831246   8255831246

22. 331476853821   331476858621   22.____
     6976658532996   6976655832996
     3766042113715   3766042113745

23. 8806663315   88066633115   23.____
     74477138449   74477138449
     211756663666   211756663666

24. 990006966996   99000696996   24._____
     53022219743   53022219843
     4171171117717   4171171177717

25. 24400222433004   24400222433004   25._____
     5300030055000355   5300030055500355
     20000075532002022   20000075532002022

26. 6111666406600001116   6111666406600001116   26._____
     7111300117001100733   7111300117001100733
     26666446664476518   26666446664476518

Questions 27-30.

DIRECTIONS: Questions 27 through 30 are to be answered by picking the answer which is in the correct numerical order, from the lowest number to the highest number, in each question.

27. A. 44533, 44518, 44516, 44547   27._____
    B. 44516, 44518, 44533, 44547
    C. 44547, 44533, 44518, 44516
    D. 44518, 44516, 44547, 44533

28. A. 95587, 95593, 95601, 95620   28._____
    B. 95601, 95620, 95587, 95593
    C. 95593, 95587, 95601. 95620
    D. 95620, 95601, 95593, 95587

29. A. 232212, 232208, 232232, 232223   29._____
    B. 232208, 232223, 232212, 232232
    C. 232208, 232212, 232223, 232232
    D. 232223, 232232, 232208, 232208

30. A. 113419, 113521, 113462, 113462   30._____
    B. 113588, 113462, 113521, 113419
    C. 113521, 113588, 113419, 113462
    D. 113419, 113462, 113521, 113588

KEY (CORRECT ANSWERS)

1.	C	11.	A	21.	C
2.	B	12.	C	22.	A
3.	D	13.	A	23.	D
4.	A	14.	A	24.	A
5.	C	15.	C	25.	C
6.	B	16.	B	26.	C
7.	D	17.	B	27.	B
8.	A	18.	B	28.	A
9.	D	19.	B	29.	C
10.	C	20.	B	30.	D

OFFICE RECORD KEEPING
EXAMINATION SECTION
TEST 1

DIRECTIONS: Each question or incomplete statement is followed by several suggested answers or completions. Select the one that BEST answers the question or completes the statement. *PRINT THE LETTER OF THE CORRECT ANSWER IN THE SPACE AT THE RIGHT.*

Questions 1-5.

DIRECTIONS: Questions 1 through 5 are to be answered on the basis of the following chart to check for address and zip code errors.

    A. No errors
    B. Address only
    C. Zip code only
    D. Both

	Correct List Address	Zip Code	List to be Checked Address	Zip Code	
1.	44-A Western Avenue Bethesda, MD	65564	44-A Western Avenue Bethesda, MD	65654	1._____
2.	567 Opera Lane Jackson, MO	28218	567 Opera Lane Jacksen, MO	28218	2._____
3.	200 W. Jannine Dr. Missoula, MT	30707	200 W. Jannine Dr. Missoula, MT	30307	3._____
4.	28 Champaline Dr. Reno, NV	34101	28 Champaine Way Reno, NV	43101	4._____
5.	65156 Rodojo Parsimony, KY	44590-7326	65156 Rodojo Parsimony, KY	44590-7326	5._____

6. When alphabetized correctly, which of the following would be second?   6._____
   A. flame   B. herring   C. decadence   D. emoticon

7. Which one of the following letters is as far after E as K is before R in the alphabet?   7._____
   A. J   B. K   C. H   D. M

8. How many pairs of the following sets of numbers are exactly alike?   8._____
    134232   123456   432512   561343
    564643   432123   132439   438318

   A. 0   B. 2   C. 3   D. 4

9. When alphabetized correctly, which of the following would be FOURTH? 9.____
   A. microcosm   B. natural   C. lithe   D. nature

10. When alphabetized correctly, which of the following would be THIRD? 10.____
    A. exoskeleton   B. euthanize   C. Europe   D. eurythmic

11. Which one of the following letters is as far before T as S is after I in the alphabet? 11.____
    A. J   B. K   C. M   D. N

12. How many pairs of the following sets of letters are exactly ALIKE? 12.____
    GIHEKE   GIHEKE
    KIWNEB   KWINEB
    PQMZJI   PMQZJI
    OPZIBS   OBZIBS
    PONEHE   POENHE

    A. 0   B. 1   C. 2   D. 4

13. When alphabetized correctly, which of the following would be FIRST? 13.____
    A. Catalina   B. catcher   C. caustic   D. curious

14. Which of the following letters is as far after D as U is after B in the alphabet? 14.____
    A. R   B. V   C. W   D. Z

Questions 15-19.

DIRECTIONS: Use the following information and chart to complete Questions 15 through 19.

Every theft reported to an adjuster needs to be assigned a six-letter code containing the following:

   First Letter: Type of theft
   Second Letter: Witnesses
   Third Letter: Value of stolen item
   Fourth Letter: Location
   Fifth Letter: Time of theft
   Sixth Letter: Elapsed between theft and report

   Type of Theft:
   A. Breaking and Entering
   B. Retail Theft
   C. Armed robbery
   D. Grand Theft Auto

   Witnesses
   A. None
   B. 1 witness
   C. Multiple witnesses
   D. Security camera

3 (#1)

Location
A. Single Family Home
B. Apartment Building
C. Store
D. Office
E. Vehicle
F. Public Space (Parking Garage, Park, etc.)

Time Elapsed Between Theft and Report
A. 0-1 hour
B. 1-4 hours
C. 4-12 hours
D. 12-24 hours
E. 24 Hours

Time of Theft
A. 7 AM – 1 PM
B. 1 PM – 6 PM
C. 6 PM – 11 PM
D. 11 PM – 3 AM
E. 3 AM – 7 AM

Value of Stolen Items
A. $0-$100
B. $101-$250
C. $251-$500
D. $500-$1000
E. $1001-$5000
F. $5000 or more

15. At 9:30 PM, $175 worth of clothing was stolen from a store. The crime was reported right away by a single store associate. Which of the following would be the CORRECT code?   15.____
    A. BCCABB   B. BBBCCA   C. ACCBAB   D. CBCABB

16. A Crossover vehicle worth $4,500 was stolen from a park at approximately 6:45 AM this morning. It was reported stolen at 11:00 AM later that morning by the owner. There were no witnesses. What is the CORRECT code?   16.____
    A. DEECAF   B. CFECAE   C. DEFECA   D. DAEFEC

17. Although it was just reported, a breaking and entering occurred 5 days ago at 1:30 AM, according to security cameras that recorded the theft at the accounting firm. Although locks and doors were damaged, nothing was stolen. Which of the following would be the CORRECT code?   17.____
    A. ADDEEA   B. ADDDAE   C. ADADDE   D. ADEADE

18. Jill Wagner was held at knifepoint this morning at 11:30 AM when she was walking out of her apartment complex. The thief demanded money, and she gave him $54. She was the only witness and reported the crime immediately. Which of the following would be the CORRECT code?   18.____
    A. CBABAA   B. BBABAA   C. CBBABB   D. ABBBCA

19. An artifact worth $5,500 was stolen from the home of Chad Judea this early evening while he was out to dinner from 5:30 PM to 6 PM. When he arrived home at 6 PM, he immediately called the police. There were no witnesses. Which of the following would be the CORRECT code?   19.____
    A. AABBAF   B. AABFAF   C. AABABF   D. AAFABA

20. Diatribe means MOST NEARLY   20.____
    A. argument   B. cooperation   C. delicate   D. arrogance

21. Vitriolic means MOST NEARLY   21.____
    A. flammable   B. fearful   C. spiteful   D. asinine

22. Aplomb means MOST NEARLY   22.____
    A. self-righteous   B. respectable   C. dispirited   D. self-confidence

23. Pervicacious means MOST NEARLY   23.____
    A. rotten   B. immoral   C. stubborn   D. immortal

24. Detrimental means MOST NEARLY   24.____
    A. valuable   B. selfish   C. hopeless   D. harmful

25. Heinous means MOST NEARLY   25.____
    A. sweating   B. glorious   C. atrocious   D. moderate

KEY (CORRECT ANSWERS)

1. C		11. A	
2. B		12. B	
3. C		13. A	
4. D		14. C	
5. A		15. B	
6. D		16. D	
7. B		17. C	
8. A		18. A	
9. D		19. D	
10. B		20. A	

21. C
22. D
23. C
24. D
25. C

TEST 2

DIRECTIONS: Each question or incomplete statement is followed by several suggested answers or completions. Select the one that BEST answers the question or completes the statement. *PRINT THE LETTER OF THE CORRECT ANSWER IN THE SPACE AT THE RIGHT.*

Questions 1-7.

DIRECTIONS: In answering Questions 1 through 7, you will be presented with analogies (known as word relationships). Select the answer choice that BEST completes the analogy.

1. Coordinated is related to movement as speech is related to 1.____
 A. predictive B. rapid C. prophetic D. articulate

2. Pottery is related to shard as wood is related to 2.____
 A. acorn B. chair C. smoke D. kiln

3. Poverty is related to money as famine is related to 3.____
 A. nourishment B. infirmity C. illness D. care

4. Farmland is related to arable as waterway is related to 4.____
 A. impenetrable B. maneuverable
 C. fertile D. deep

5. 19 is related to 17 as 37 is related to 5.____
 A. 39 B. 36 C. 34 D. 31

6. Cup is related to lip as bird is related to 6.____
 A. beak B. grass C. forest D. bush

7. ZRYQ is related to KCJB as PWOV is related to 7.____
 A. GBHA B. ISJT C. ELDK D. EOFP

Questions 8-12.

DIRECTIONS: In answering Questions 8 through 12, each of the questions has a group. Find out which one of the given alternatives will be another member of that group.

8. Springfield, Sacramento, Tallahassee 8.____
 A. Buffalo B. Bangor C. Pittsburgh D. Providence

9. Lock, Shut, Fasten 9.____
 A. Window B. Iron C. Door D. Block

10. Pathology, Radiology, Ophthalmology 10.____
 A. Zoology B. Hematology C. Geology D. Biology

135

11. Karate, Jujitsu, Boxing 11.____
    A. Polo B. Pole-vault C. Judo D. Swimming

12. Newspaper, Hoarding, Television 12.____
    A. Press B. Rumor C. Media D. Broadcast

Questions 13-18.

DIRECTIONS: Questions 13 through 18 are to be answered on the basis of the following pie chart.

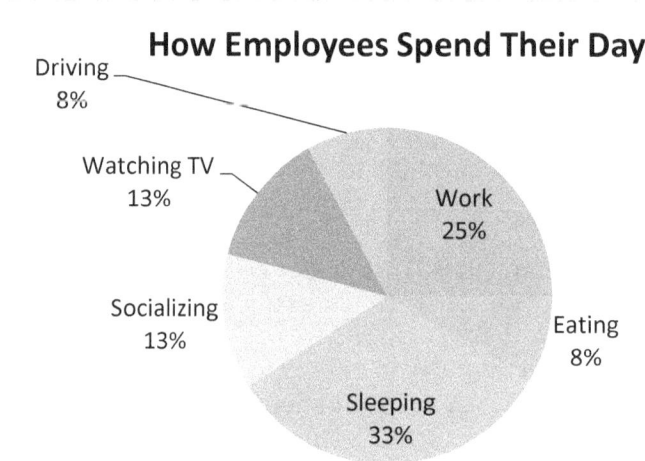

How Employees Spend Their Days

- Driving 8%
- Watching TV 13%
- Socializing 13%
- Sleeping 33%
- Eating 8%
- Work 25%

13. Approximately how many hours a day are spent eating? 13.____
    A. 2 hours B. 5 hours C. 1 hour D. 30 minutes

14. According to the graph, for each 48 hour period, about how many hours are spent socializing and watching TV? 14.____
    A. 9 hours B. 6 hours C. 12 hours D. 3 hours

15. If an employee ate two-thirds of their meals at a restaurant, what percentage of the total day is spent eating at home? 15.____
    A. 2.5% B. 5.3% C. 8% D. 1.4%

16. About how many hours a day are spent working and sleeping? 16.____
    A. 7 B. 10 C. 12 D. 14

17. Which of the following equations could be used to figure out how much time an employee spends watching TV during a week? T equals the total amount of time watching TV during the week. 17.____
    A. T = 13% x 24 x 7 B. T = 24 x 13 x 7
    C. T = 24/13% x 7 D. T = 1.3 x 7 x 24

18. How many hours a week does the average employee spend socializing? 18.____
    A. 20 B. 22 C. 23 D. 24

Questions 19-25.

DIRECTIONS: Questions 19 through 25 are to be answered on the basis of the following charts.

DIAL DIRECT	WEEKDAY FULL RATE		EVENING 40% DISCOUNT		WEEKEND 60% DISCOUNT	
SAMPLE RATES FROM SEATTLE TO	FIRST MINUTE	EACH ADDITIONAL MINUTE	FIRST MINUTE	EACH ADDITIONAL MINUTE	FIRST MINUTE	EACH ADDITIONAL MINUTE
Savannah, GA	.52	.23	.31	.14	.21	.08
Providence, RI	.52	.223	.31	.14	.21	.08
Golden, CO	.52	.23	.31	.14	.21	.08
Indianapolis, IN	.48	.19	.29	.11	.19	.07
San Diego, CA	.54	.24	.32	.14	.22	.09
Tallahassee, FL	.54	.24	.32	.14	.22	.09
Milwaukee, WI	.57	.27	.34	.16	.23	.09
Minneapolis, MN	.49	.22	.29	.13	.20	.08
Baton Rouge, LA	.52	.23	.31	.14	.21	.08
Buffalo, NY	.52	.23	.31	.14	.21	.08
Annapolis, MD	.54	.24	.32	.14	.22	.09
Washington, DC	.52	.23	.31	.14	.21	.08

OPERATOR ASSISTED		
STATION-TO-STATION		PERSON-TO-PERSON
1 – 10 MILES	$.75	$3.00 FEE FOR ALL MILEAGES
11 - 22 MILES	$1.10	*NOTE: Add to this base charge – the minute rates from the above chart
23-3000 MILES	$1.55	

19. What is the price of a 6-minute dial direct call to Annapolis, MD when you call on a weekend?
    A. $0.59 B. $0.54 C. $0.67 D. $0.49

19.____

20. What is the difference in cost between a 10 minute dial direct to Buffalo, NY and a 10 minute person-to-person call to Buffalo, NY?
    A. $1.55 B. $3.00 C. $0.55 D. $4.55

20.____

21. What is the price of a 15-minute operator-assisted Station-to-Station call to Indianapolis, IN on a Monday at noon?
    A. $3.74 B. $7.80 C. $3.45 D. $4.69

21.____

22. What is the difference in price between an 11-minute dial direct call to Milwaukee, WI at 11:00 AM on a Wednesday and the same call made at 9 PM that night?
    A. $2.27 B. $3.00 C. $1.55 D. $1.336

22.____

23. Which of the following is NOT a type of charge for a dial direct call? 23._____
    A. Holiday   B. Evening   C. Weekend   D. Weekday

24. If a 3.5% tax applied to the total cost of any call, what would be the TOTAL cost of a 13-minute weekday, dial direct call to Golden, CO? 24._____
    A. $3.28   B. $3.39   C. $4.94   D. $6.39

25. What is the amount of discount from a dial direct, weekday call to Tallahassee, FL cost as compared to a dial direct, weekend call to Tallahassee? 25._____
    A. 45%   B. 30%   C. 60%   D. 20%

KEY (CORRECT ANSWERS)

1.	D	11.	C
2.	B	12.	D
3.	A	13.	A
4.	C	14.	C
5.	D	15.	A
6.	A	16.	D
7.	C	17.	A
8.	D	18.	B
9.	D	19.	C
10.	B	20.	B

21.	D
22.	D
23.	A
24.	B
25.	C

TEST 3

DIRECTIONS: Each question or incomplete statement is followed by several suggested answers or completions. Select the one that BEST answers the question or completes the statement. *PRINT THE LETTER OF THE CORRECT ANSWER IN THE SPACE AT THE RIGHT.*

Questions 1-7.

DIRECTIONS: Questions 1 through 7 are to be answered on the basis of the following graph.

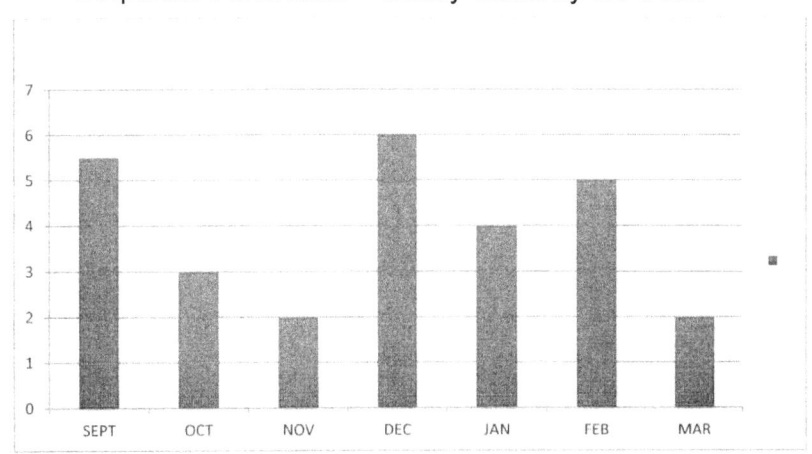

1. The vertical scale ranging from 0 to 7 represents the number of
   A. students selling candy
   B. candy sold in each case
   C. days each month that candy was sold
   D. cases of candy sold

   1.____

2. Which two months had approximately the same amount of candy sold?
   A. November and March
   B. September and February
   C. November and October
   D. October and March

   2.____

3. Which month showed a 100% increase in sales over the month of November?
   A. March   B. January   C. April   D. December

   3.____

4. From month-to-month, which month saw an approximate 33% drop in sales from the previous month?
   A. March   B. September   C. January   D. October

   4.____

5. The amount of candy sold in December is twice the amount of candy sold in which other month?
   A. October   B. March   C. January   D. September

   5.____

139

6. What was the total amount of candy sold during the months shown on the graph?
   A. 44 cases   B. 35.5 cases   C. 23.5 cases   D. 27.5 cases

7. If the fundraiser extended the additional five months of the year and added an additional 65% in sales, approximately how many cases would be sold in total for an entire year?
   A. 40.5 cases   B. 37 cases   C. 45 cases   D. 27.5 cases

Questions 8-11.

DIRECTIONS: Questions 8 through 11 are to be answered on the basis of the following chart.

S = 10 students
s = 5 students

Mr. Hucklebee	S S S S s
Ms. Shopenhauer	S S S
Mr. White	S S S s
Mrs. Mulrooney	S S S

8. The size of Mr. White's class is _____ students.
   A. 30   B. 35   C. 40   D. 4

9. The total of all students in all four classes is _____ students.
   A. 150   B. 140   C. 125   D. 14

10. The average class size based on the above chart is _____ students.
    A. 140   B. 45   C. 35   D. 30

11. In order to ensure each teacher has the same amount of students in each class, how many students would need to transfer out of Mr. Hucklebee's class?
    A. 10
    B. 5
    C. 0
    d. 15 would need to transfer into his class

12. When alphabetized correctly, which of the following would be THIRD?
    A. box   B. departed   C. electrical   D. elemental

13. When alphabetized correctly, which of the following would be SECOND?
    A. polarize   B. omnipotent   C. polygraph   D. omniscient

14. When alphabetized correctly, which of the following would be THIRD?
    A. Macklemore, Jonathan   B. Mackelmore, J.
    C. DiCastro, Darian   D. Castro, Darren Henry

15. The group fought through the fog, *shambling* through the night, doing their best to stay upright.
    The word *shambling* means
    A. frozen in place   B. running
    C. walking awkwardly   D. shivering uncontrollably

    15.____

16. Many doctors agree that Gen-aspirin is the best for fighting headaches. It comes in different flavors and is easy to swallow.
    Is this a valid or invalid argument?
    A. Invalid   B. Valid

    16.____

Questions 17-21.

DIRECTIONS: Questions 17 through 21 are to be answered on the basis of the following paragraph.

Hospital workers and volunteers often ask Mr. Ansley to educate children who are hospitalized with primary ciliary dyskinesia (PCD). As he goes through the precautionary cleaning process (scrubbing, donning sterilized clothes, etc.) in order to see his students, Mr. Ansley wonders why their parents add the stress and pressure of schooling and trying to play catch-up because of the amount of time spent in the hospital and not in the classroom, which is an unfortunate side effect of patients with PCD. These children go through so many painful treatments on a given day that it seems punishing to subject them to schooling as normal children do, especially with life expectancy being as short as it is.

17. What is meant by *precautionary* in the second sentence?
    A. Careful   B. Protective   C. Sterilizing   D. Medical

    17.____

18. What is the MAIN idea of this passage?
    A. The preparation to visit a patient with primary ciliary dyskinesia is extensive.
    B. Children with PCD are unable to live normal lives.
    C. Children with PCD die young.
    D. Certain allowances should be made for children with PCD.

    18.____

19. What is the author's purpose?
    A. To advise   B. To educate
    C. To establish credibility   D. To amuse

    19.____

20. What is the author's tone?
    A. Cruel   B. Sympathetic
    C. Disbelieving   D. Cheerful

    20.____

21. How is Mr. Ansley so familiar with the procedures used when visiting a child with PCD?
    A. He has read about it
    B. He works in the hospital.
    C. His child has PCD.
    D. He tutors them on a regular basis.

    21.____

Questions 22-25.

DIRECTIONS: One of the underlined words in Questions 22 through 25 should be changed. Select the one that should be changed and print the letter of the word that would change the underlined word.

22. After we washed the fruit that had growing in the garden, we knew there was a store that would buy them.
 A. washing B. grown C. is D. No change

 22.____

23. When the temperature drops under 32 degrees (F), the water on the lake freezes, which allowed children to skate across it.
 A. dropped B. froze C. allows D. No change

 23.____

24. My friend's bulldog, while chasing cars in the street, always manages to knock over our garbage bins.
 A. chased B. manage C. knocks D. No change

 24.____

25. Some of the ice on the driveway has melted.
 A. having melted B. have melted
 C. has melt D. No change

 25.____

KEY (CORRECT ANSWERS)

1.	D	11.	A
2.	A	12.	C
3.	B	13.	D
4.	C	14.	B
5.	A	15.	C
6.	D	16.	A
7.	C	17.	C
8.	B	18.	D
9.	B	19.	A
10.	C	20.	B

21. D
22. B
23. C
24. D
25. D

TEST 4

DIRECTIONS: Each question or incomplete statement is followed by several suggested answers or completions. Select the one that BEST answers the question or completes the statement. *PRINT THE LETTER OF THE CORRECT ANSWER IN THE SPACE AT THE RIGHT.*

Questions 1-2.

DIRECTIONS: One of the underlined words in Questions 1 and 2 should be changed. Select the one that should be changed and print the letter of the word that would change the underlined word.

1. You can get to Martha's Vineyard by driving from Boston to Woods Hole. Once there, you can travel over on a boat, but you may find traveling by airplane to be more exciting.
   A. they   B. visitors   C. it   D. No change

   1.____

2. When John wants to go to the store looking for milk and eggs, you must remember to bring his wallet.
   A. them   B. he   C. its   D. No change

   2.____

3. An item that sells for $400 is put on sale at $145. What is the percentage of decrease?
   A. 25%   B. 28%   C. 64%   D. 36%

   3.____

4. Two Junior College Mathematics courses have a total of 510 students. The 9:00 AM class has 60 more than the 12:30 PM class. How many students are in the 12:30 class?
   A. 225   B. 285   C. 255   D. 205

   4.____

5. If a car gets 26 miles per gallon and it has driven 75,210 miles, approximately what is the number of gallons of gas that it has used?
   A. 3,000   B. 2,585   C. 165   D. 1,800

   5.____

6. Which one of the following sentences about proper telephone usage is NOT always correct? When answering a telephone, you should
   A. know who you are speaking to
   B. give the caller your undivided attention
   C. identify yourself to the caller
   D. obtain the information your caller wishes before you do other work

   6.____

143

7. You are part of the "Safety at Work" committee, which is dedicated to ensuring safety of employees. During your regular shift, you notice an employee in violation of one of your committee's rules. Which of the following actions should you take FIRST?
   A. Speak with the employee about the safety rules and mandate them to stop breaking the rules.
   B. Speak to the employee about safety rules and point out the rule they violated.
   C. Bring up the issue during the next committee meeting.
   D. Report the violation to the employee's superiors.

7.____

8. Part of your duties is overseeing employee confidential information. A friend and coworker of yours asks to obtain information concerning another employee. Which is the BEST action to take?
   A. Ask the coworker if you can share the information.
   B. Ask your supervisor if you can give the information to your friend.
   C. Refuse to give the information to your friend.
   D. Give the information to your friend.

8.____

9. Which of the following words means the OPPOSITE of protract?
   A. Extend   B. Hesitant   C. Curtail   D. Plethora

9.____

10. Which of the following words means the OPPOSITE of conserve?
    A. Relinquish   B. Waste   C. Proficient   D. Rigid

10.____

11. Which of the following words means the SAME as dissipate?
    A. Scatter   B. Emancipate
    C. Engage   D. Accumulate

11.____

12. Your office just purchased 14 fax machines. Each fax machine costs $79.99. How much did the 14 fax machines cost?
    A. $1,119.86   B. $1,108.77   C. $1,201.44   D. $1,788.22

12.____

Questions 13-19.

DIRECTIONS: Questions 13 through 19 are to be answered on the basis of the following chart.

Office City	Sales Rank	Production Materials Produced	Rank for Production	Damaged Materials	Employees	Percent of Profit	Sales Points	Weeks Without Injuries
Springfield	13.6	271	12	1	34	35	36	7
Philadelphia	17	274	4	3	25	41	20	4
Gary	16	260	10	5	34	34	21	3
Boulder	5	10	6	9	38	15	20	8
Miami	81	3	81	77	133	4	2	0
Houston	2	370	2	0	95	66	100	16
Battle Creek	82	290	82	81	91	13	9	2

13. Between Philadelphia and Battle Creek, how many damaged materials were there?   13.____
    A. 84   B. 78   C. 45   D. 86

14. How many offices have had 5 or more weeks without injuries?   14.____
    A. 3   B. 4   C. 2   D. 0

15. What was the TOTAL number of damaged materials for the offices in Boulder, Miami, Houston, and Springfield offices?   15.____
    A. 91   B. 87   C. 80   D. 77

16. What were the TOTAL sales points of Houston, Battle Creek, and Gary?   16.____
    A. 115   B. 145   C. 160   D. 130

17. Which of the offices had the LOWEST number of weeks without an injury?   17.____
    A. Battle Creek   B. Miami   C. Gary   D. Philadelphia

18. If worker efficiency is a percentage based on the number of workers at an office and the amount of materials produced, which office has the GREATEST worker efficiency?   18.____
    A. Philadelphia   B. Springfield   C. Boulder   D. Gary

19. If the company was looking to close a facility, which of the following factors would NOT be a reason to close the Miami office?   19.____
    A. Weeks without injury   B. Sales rank
    C. Production materials produced   D. Employees

Questions 20-25.

DIRECTIONS: In answering Questions 20 through 25, select the sentence in which the underlined word is used correctly.

20. A. Jon needs to increase his <u>capitol</u> by 30% to invest in my business.   20.____
    B. The organization is reevaluating <u>it's</u> decision to purchase the building.
    C. The office supply store sells computer paper and <u>stationery</u>.
    D. The quarterback and running back left <u>there</u> helmets on the bus.

21. A. The police sergeant <u>sited</u> me for disorderly conduct and driving without a license.   21.____
    B. The votes have <u>already</u> been counted.
    C. The professor's theory contradicts the <u>principals</u> of Einstein and Newton.
    D. <u>Who's</u> glass of water is on the table?

22. A. The board of trustees decided to <u>accept</u> the CEO's resignation.   22.____
    B. <u>Lose</u> hats will help keep your head from hurting.
    C. She <u>complemented</u> me on my exquisite dinner tastes.
    D. Jamaal offered him some sound <u>advise</u>.

23. A. In class today, Maya lead us in the reciting of the pledge. 23._____
    B. Doctors worry about the affects of drinking red wine right before bed.
    C. The workers used sledge hammers to break up the pavement.
    D. The teacher gave her students wise council.

24. A. This building was formerly the site of one of the city's oldest department stores. 24._____
    B. In his position, Albert must be very discrete in handling confidential information.
    C. He was to tired to continue the race.
    D. Each of his mortgage payments as about evenly divided between principle and interest.

25. A. The police spent several hours at the cite of the accident. 25._____
    B. A majority of the public support capitol punishment.
    C. The magician used mirrors to create a convincing illusion.
    D. The heiress flouted her wealth by wearing expensive jewelry.

KEY (CORRECT ANSWERS)

1.	D	11.	A
2.	B	12.	A
3.	C	13.	A
4.	A	14.	A
5.	A	15.	B
6.	D	16.	D
7.	B	17.	B
8.	C	18.	A
9.	C	19.	D
10.	B	20.	C

21.	B
22.	A
23.	C
24.	A
25.	C

EXAMINATION SECTION

TEST 1

DIRECTIONS: Each sentence contains one error in spelling, diction, or grammar which may be corrected by changing one word. Underline the faulty word and write your correction in the first column opposite the sentence. Then, in the second column, write C if the sentence is correctly punctuated, F if the sentence has faulty punctuation. Make the necessary change in punctuation in the typed sentence.

		CORRECTION	PUNCTUATION
1.	Neither of the books, which Miss Smith suggested, are available at the library.		
2.	Many a typist writing in haste has mispelled "benefited."		
3.	Mr. Ames, together with his two sons, attend church every Sunday; their regularity, in fact, is almost unbelievable.		
4.	Although I agree with you on most subjects, I differ from you on this question.		
5.	My new duties are different than my former ones, however, I infer from your comments that I am giving satisfaction.		
6.	ABC, a local textile firm, is employing two of our students—Mary and I.		
7.	Which of your friends writes to you most often Edith or Anne?		
8.	The new of Ann and John getting married came as a complete surprise to us.		
9.	Rachel, Mary, and Mrs. Mason, have all announced that their going to the meeting.		
10.	The supervisor, who gave the report, referred to data which has been collected in the file.		
11.	If I was in your place—and I'm sorry I'm not—I'd do just what you plan to do in this matter.		

12. Miss Jones, the Supervisor of Files, has said said that we have less folders in use than we should have.

13. The E Company which is now located on Seventh Avenue, will build their new office building on Fifth Avenue.

14. It was Lee and me, not you and she, who planned this meeting.

15. I expect everyone but me to have their plans finished by Thursday, mine will keep me busy until next week.

16. The Committee, having arrived at it's decision, adjourned the meeting.

17. A young woman, together with three cats, a dog, and a parakeet, live in a nearby apartment.

18. One of the typists or bookkeepers, must have dropped their cigarette on the floor.

19. Three plural possessives which give many people trouble are: ladies' boys', and thiefs'.

20. Neither Mrs. Blake nor her daughter has swam in the ocean all summer; though each is a good swimmer.

21. The boys and the girls go in the building through separate entrances.

22. The lawyer advised his client to accept the altared contract, but the suggestion was ignored.

23. Occasionally a series of tests are given for the benefit of personnel, who seek promotion.

24. Don't anyone here know the correct date?

25. A new, well-planned, sketch lead us to our own office.

KEY (CORRECT ANSWERS)

CORRECTION	PUNCTUATION
1. Underline are; replace by is	1. F (remove commas (,) after books and after suggested)
2. Underline mispelled; replace by misspelled	2. C
3. Underline attend; replace by attends	3. C
4. Underline from; replace by with	4. C
5. Underline than; replace by from	5. F (remove comma (,) after ones; replace by semicolon (;)
6. Underline I; replace by me	6. C
7. Underline most; replace by more	7. F (add comma (,) after often)
8. Underline John; replace by John's	8. C
9. Underline their; replace by they're	9. F (remove comma (,) after Mason)
10. Underline has; replace by have	10. F (remove comma (,) after supervisor and after report)
11. Underline was; replace by were	11. C
12. Underline less; replace by fewer	12. C
13. Underline their; replace by its	13. F (place comma (,) after Company)
14. Underline me; replace by I	14. C
15. Underline their; replace by his	15. F (remove comma (,) after Thursday; replace by semicolon (;))
16. Underline it's; replace by its	16. C
17. Underline live; replace by lives	17. C
18. Underline their; replace by his	18. F (remove comma (,) after bookkeepers)
19. Underline thiefs'; replace by thieves'	19. F (place comma (,) after ladies')

4 (#1)

20. Underline swam; replace by swum
20. F (remove semicolon (;) after summer; replace by comma (,))

21. Underline in; replace by into
21. C

22. Underline altared; replace by altered
22. C

23. Underline are; replace by is
23. F (remove comma (,) after personnel)

24 Underline Don't; replace by Doesn't
24. C

25. Underline lead; replace by led
25. F (remove comma (,) after well-planned)

TEST 2

DIRECTIONS: Each sentence contains one error in spelling, diction, or grammar which may be corrected by changing one word. Underline the faulty word and write your correction in the first column opposite the sentence. Then, in the second column, write C if the sentence is correctly punctuated, F if the sentence has faulty punctuation. Make the necessary change in punctuation in the typed sentence.

		CORRECTION	PUNCTUATION
1.	The girls have gone to the meeting, their papers laying about the desk.		
2.	There seems to be more people here than I expected, but others are still arriving.		
3.	The reason I went home yesterday was because I was ill; I am glad to say, that I am better now.		
4.	I saw on the bulletin board where the meeting, scheduled for tomorrow, has been postponed.		
5.	Will the new regulations have any affect upon our routine?		
6.	Each of today's reports, according to this statement, have been filled in duplicate.		
7.	In order to avoid embarassment, we must keep this matter in confidence, between you and me.		
8.	Miss X called Ellen and I to her office, because we were to be commended for punctuality.		
9.	The officer has occasionally objected to my boss parking his car in front of the office.		
10.	The girl dresses well, furthermore, she looks irresistable.		
11.	American business, if we may believe the <u>Wall Street Journal</u>, operate on the principal of free competition.		

12. The fine climate and the beautiful scenery of New York State, attracts tourists from all over the country.

13. Stenographers, who have trouble with spelling often refer to the dictionary continuously.

14. I was amazed—you know this without me telling you—when I heard the news about you.

15. The records show that most every employee has made suggestions for work improvement.

16. The traffic signal changed, as they past the corner.

17. John said that he did not know if he would accept the invitation or not, but I think he will.

18. I do not know as I can persuade her to see the matter in this light, however, I will try,

19. I thought the weather looked some better this morning; the newspaper, however, says we may expect another hot, humid day.

20. The employment manager eliminated her from consideration because of Ethel being under eighteen.

21. Every one of the girls, who were lucky enough to see the parade, have been giving a glowing account of it,

22. Mary Jones's brother is taller than her, although he is only thirteen years old.

23. When the news report came in everyone in the room was quietly reading to themselves.

24. The thing visitors to New York first notice is the heighth of the buildings.

25. Whom do you expect to see if not Charles and I.

3 (#2)

KEY (CORRECT ANSWERS)

CORRECTION	PUNCTUATION
1. Underline laying; replace by lying	1. C
2. Underline seems; replace by seem	2. C
3. Underline was; replace by is	3. F (remove comma (,) after say)
4. Underline where; replace by that	4. F (remove commas (,) after meeting and after tomorrow)
5. Underline affect; replace by effect	5. C
6. Underline have; replace by has	6. C
7. Underline embarassment; replace by embarrassment	7. F (remove comma (,) after confidence)
8. Underline I; replace by me	8. F (remove comma (,) after office)
9. Underline boss; replace by boss's	9. F (remove commas (,) after has and after occasionally)
10. Underline irresistable; replace by irresistible	10. F (remove comma (,) after well; replace by semicolon (;))
11. Underline principal; replace by principle	11. C
12. Underline attracts; replace by attract	12. F (remove comma) (,) after State)
13. Underline continuously; replace by continually	13. F (place commas (,) after Stenographers and after spelling)
14. Underline me; replace by my	14. C
15. Underline most; replace by almost	15. C
16. Underline past; replace by passed	16. F (remove comma (,) after changed)
17. Underline if; replace by whether	17. C
18. Underline as; replace by whether	18. F (remove comma (,) after light; replace by semicolon (;))
19. Underline some; replace by somewhat	19. C

4 (#2)

20. Underline Ethel; replace by Ethel's

21. Underline have; replace by has

22. Underline her; replace by she

23. Underline themselves; replace by himself

24. Underline heighth; replace by height

25. Underline I; replace by me

20. C

21. F (remove commas (,) after girls and after parade)

22. F (remove comma (,) after her she)

23. F (place comma (,) after came in)

24. C

25. F (place question mark (?) after I (me))

www.ingramcontent.com/pod-product-compliance
Lightning Source LLC
Chambersburg PA
CBHW080735230426
43665CB00020B/2741